KURT
FORCING THE EDGE

KURT
FORCING THE EDGE

KURT BROWNING
WITH NEIL STEVENS

HarperCollins*Publishers*Ltd

KURT: FORCING THE EDGE. Copyright © 1991 by Kurt Browning Enterprises Inc. All rights reserved. No part of this book may be used or reproduced in any manner whatsoever without prior written permission except in the case of brief quotations embodied in reviews. For information address HarperCollins Publishers Ltd, Suite 2900, 55 Avenue Road, Toronto, Canada M5R 3L2.

First Edition

Canadian Cataloguing in Publication Data

Browning, Kurt, 1966-
    Kurt: forcing the edge

ISBN 0-00-215843-4

1. Browning, Kurt, 1966- . 2. Skaters — Canada — Biography. I. Stevens, Neil, 1947- . II. Title.

GV850.B7A3 1991   796.91'2'092   C91-095213-2

91 92 93 94 95 AG 5 4 3 2 1

To my parents and my family who were always there for me—and to anyone who has ever enjoyed stepping out on something slippery.

CONTENTS

Forcing the Edge

In skating terms, forcing the edge means you are pushing against the natural running edge of your blade, causing you to look awkward and lose your momentum.

In my terms, forcing the edge means something entirely different. Pushing yourself beyond your limit, working the edge of the envelope, skating to the edge of disaster. In other words . . . PUSHING YOUR LUCK!

—K.B.

INTRODUCTION

My cousin Kurt was only a year old and had just learned how to walk.

The concrete sidewalk in front of our house in Clive, Alberta, was about four inches higher than the lawn. Kurt, in diaper and rubber pants, decided to take the big step up.

Balancing himself on one chubby leg, he carefully lifted the other but lost his balance and toppled over. He got up and tried again, only to fall to the concrete on his knees. Again he tried, and again he failed. His knees were skinned and his hands made a cold slap every time they connected with the sidewalk. But he wouldn't quit.

He was angry—not because of the physical pain, but because he couldn't do what he wanted to. Tears of frustration ran down his cheeks.

He tried yet again. He wobbled but he made it. We

cheered and applauded. He turned to look at us with a big smile on his face. Then he toddled off to an even bigger challenge—a twelve-inch step down to the driveway. His mother, Neva, put a stop to that one.

As you can see, Kurt was born with a fierce determination to succeed. He set his sights high, and he always followed through and finished whatever he attempted.

When Kurt left home at sixteen to train in Edmonton, he moved into an apartment with me and his brother Wade. This was long before he'd won a major competition. But even so, there was a sense of destiny in what he was doing at the Royal Glenora Club, where he spent so many long hours practicing jumps and polishing his footwork. He would come home each night and tell me about his progress. Every time something special happened, we'd look at each other and one of us would say, "That's going to be in the book."

We were half-joking, but half-serious, too. It wasn't conceit or an inflated ego. It was just the way Kurt was— and still is. He knew he had natural ability, and he was willing to put in the time and effort necessary to develop his skill. He seemed to know that he was going to do something very special someday.

Now, he's a three-time world champion, preparing for his biggest challenges yet—the 1992 Winter Olympics in Albertville, France, and the next world championships, in Oakland, California.

We'll all be cheering him on. And if fate deals him a bad hand, we'll love him anyway.

But I'm betting on Kurt. If anybody can do it, he can.

Put that in the book.

—Jennifer Grant, Kurt's cousin
Summer 1991

1

THE KID FROM CAROLINE

Did you ever feel that you couldn't breathe, no matter how you tried? That's exactly how I felt that day. My heart was pounding so hard I thought it was going to bounce out of my chest. I was standing at center ice, wondering what could possibly be taking so long; it doesn't take forever to put a tape into a machine. Then, suddenly, the music started without me, and I had to hurry to catch up.

I didn't have much in the way of a master plan. My coach had thrown together a series of daring moves at the very last minute and we'd practiced them once, the day before. Once I got in motion, I wasn't quite so nervous. It was my turn; I could handle that. Away I went.

I was moving fast, listening to the music and enjoying myself a little bit too much. I went into a spin—my first mistake. The spins gave me time to think, which was always dangerous. I came out of it and stepped into my next move, which wasn't there. I'd gone completely blank. But, being full of guile, I reasoned that if I glided around for a bit, it would occur to me. No such luck. I had no idea what came next.

I couldn't disappoint all those people sitting in the stands, so I began to wing it. I hadn't done an Axel yet, so I threw one in. Terrific—the crowd seemed to appreciate it. Maybe they'd like another spin as well. Why not? I sailed on with an original Kurt Browning creation, never to be seen again. My arms and legs were going in all directions, but I was having a wonderful time. I was eleven years old, the toast of the Lacombe Arena, about to be judged the third-best pre-juvenile male skater in all of central Alberta.

That weekend, I was sitting on a set of swings with a friend named Darwin Wren. I told him about my bronze medal, safe on the mantelpiece at home. He was less than overwhelmed, and I don't blame him—it meant that I'd come third in a field of six. But I was in my glory. It was the first time I'd ever won anything, and I liked the sensation, even though I hadn't a clue where it might lead.

People ask me, in all seriousness, when I realized that all manner of incredible stuff was going to happen to me. My father has the answer to that. He says that being a figure skater's parent "comes on you gradual, like being choked by smoke." Believe me, the skies don't open. No light shines down and points the way. It's not like *Field of Dreams*; there's no voice that says, "If you build a rink, he will skate." Dad would have remembered that. My skating was a natural thing, a part of growing up. I had no idea that fourteen years later I'd still be at it, loving every minute. No one could have guessed that, instead of bragging to my friend on a playground swing, I'd be on a world-wide roller-coaster ride, with millions of people watching my every move.

Right now, I can sit on the porch and look straight ahead to the south, out beyond the pasture to where the spruce and poplars stand tall along the Clearwater River. To the right, I can see the Rocky Mountains, rising from the foothills against a brilliant sky. This is where I grew up, on a country road five miles outside Caroline, Alberta, population 389. This is the place I still think of as home.

Jasper Browning, my great-grandfather, arrived in the region in 1906 with five children and a covered wagon. He'd been a sheriff in the Oklahoma Territory (I wish we had the badge he must have worn). His wife had passed away, and he'd decided to make a new start, by homesteading a section of untamed western wilderness.

Scraping out a living was difficult. Twice he packed up and crossed the border back to the United States; twice he thought better of it and returned. His kids grew up and established themselves around the countryside. One of them, Jack Browning, settled near Caroline and married Gladys Stewart in 1921. That same year, their first child was born. His name was Arnold, but Jack had a dog named Dewey, and the nickname migrated to his son. (I never thought of Dad as an Arnold. The only Arnold I knew about ran a burger joint on the TV program "Happy Days.") Two other children, Dick and Thelma, came later on.

Meanwhile, another couple from Montana, Fred and Bernice Hart, had arrived in 1913 and begun to farm a section of their own. They would have five children: Ralph, Elmer, Marjorie, Doris and (finally) Neva, born in 1925. The two families met and began visiting back and forth. At that time, the Caroline area was still a semi-wilderness, with no electricity, telephones or paved roads. Jack Browning earned good money by guiding government crews on topographical surveys, packing up horses and leading the

5

map-makers into the mountains. These trips revealed an amazing variety of wildlife—deer and elk, bighorn sheep, cougar, grizzlies and timber wolves. Hunters were taking an interest in the region, and Jack decided to augment his income by starting an outfitting business. He and a friend placed advertisements in *Field and Stream* magazine. Pretty soon, well-to-do American sportsmen began showing up on the Browning doorstep.

By this time, Dewey was a teenager, ready to help them with the expeditions. It was seasonal work, so everyone juggled a variety of jobs, from running traplines to felling trees for the lumber companies. Dewey also made his name on the rodeo circuit. He was a pickup man, the guy who rode alongside the bronco riders. Dewey grabbed the bucking horse by its halter while the rider grabbed Dewey's waist and slid safely to the ground.

Pretty soon, it became clear to everyone that Dewey and Neva Hart were more than friends. But when she moved to Calgary and worked in a bank for two years, their courtship became long-distance. Dewey persisted, writing her letters and making himself irresistible when she came home for holidays. Finally, he popped the question, and they married in 1947. He was twenty-five; she was twenty-two. They bought a 160-acre farm from Dewey's father—part of the 325-acre property they own today—and started life together in a log house, before building the one I was raised in.

Twice they nearly moved to the United States, like my Great-grandfather Jasper. In 1948, Neva's relatives in Wyoming invited them to buy a ranch, but Dewey didn't like the look of the land. Then, two years later, relatives who lived in Montana and worked at a golf course and country club persuaded Dewey to take on the caretaker's job. He and Neva applied for U.S. citizenship, only to be told that they'd submitted the wrong forms. Dewey had a low tolerance for red tape and paperwork. As a result, the band plays "O Canada" instead of "The Star Spangled Banner" when I'm on the podium.

Dewey and Neva had been married eight years when Wade was born, in 1955. My sister Dena came along three years later. Then, after what you might call a waiting period, there was me, on June 18, 1966. Mom told me that I was conceived during an autumn hunting trip along the Clearwater. She was into her forties, suddenly pregnant again. To tell you the truth, I was more or less an accident.

Growing up in Caroline, I was never conscious of the fact my father was a cowboy. Mind you, when I got on the figure-skating circuit, I noticed that he was a little different from the other dads. Till then, he was just my dad. They don't really look alike, but he always reminded me of Matt Dillon from "Gunsmoke," except that Dad isn't just a TV cowboy—he's the real thing, even though the way of life he dreamed and lived is just about gone forever. Traveling and growing, learning from new people and seeing other lands has made me a bit bigger inside. But I don't forget what I was, what my mom and dad were, and always will be.

What was it like growing up in Caroline? My pets were bloodhounds, horses and cattle. I had my first horse when I was four. Her name was Sham. I loved that big old mare.

I remember sitting around the kitchen table when the American hunters would arrive, talking in mysterious southern drawls about life in Louisiana or Kentucky.

Wade is eleven years older than I am, so when he moved to Edmonton to attend school I was only four. He'd be back home on weekends and holidays. I always looked forward to his visits. He had a full social life. If he was heading for a dance, I'd ask him, "Wade, where you going?" And he'd answer, "Crazy." "When you going to come back?" I'd ask. And he'd reply, "When I'm done." We went through this little dialogue every time.

I remember starting school, walking down the lane to wait for the bus with my sister Dena. We'd do what every kid does who has to stand and wait for a bus—shuffle along making lines in the snow, throw rocks, daydream and spend what seemed like hours watching clouds. Dena didn't always have much patience with me. I was very active and could be a royal pain.

I looked up to Dena, who was very smart, and very athletic, too. She was on all the school teams. She used to trick me into fetching her javelin when she was practicing for the Alberta Summer Games. She turned it into a contest, and I fell for it every time. She'd throw the javelin about half a mile, and I'd bust my butt, running to see how quickly I could retrieve it. The more we did this, the better she got, and I felt a tiny bit responsible when she won the competition.

Pretty soon it was Dena's turn to leave home, to attend university in Edmonton. I was only nine, and after she left, I was on my own. The plus side was that I got more than my share of my parents' attention.

It was a mile and a half up the road to my nearest friend's house. Gavin Trimble and I would spend hours riding bikes. We'd meet halfway and head on out from there. His dad worked as an outfitter and guide like mine.

There were lots of times when both our dads were gone to the hills for weeks at a time. We were very proud of them. One of our favorite things was to sit in a corner and listen to the stories they told with their friends. When they came home from an expedition, Dad's beard would have grown out. It wasn't stubble, it was a wire brush. The first thing he'd do would be to greet me with a whisker kiss, rubbing his hairy old face all over my cheeks. I must have liked it, though, because I was always first out of the house to welcome him back.

Sometimes Dad took me with him on the trapline, pointing out tracks in the mud or snow. He wouldn't say anything, just point. This was my cue to name the animal, from rabbits to elk and deer. Back home, we'd skin beaver and muskrat for their pelts. These animals were part of our everyday survival; we needed the money the pelts brought. But taking only what we needed was a fundamental rule. I never shot a deer or elk; I was always along just for the ride.

There were almost always cattle on the farm, along with the milk cows. Cozy was my favorite; Black Dancer would put her foot into the bucket after you'd spent half an hour filling it. Once, Gavin and I helped deliver a calf, just like Billy Crystal in the movie *City Slickers*, except that we used a rope and a hockey stick. I'm fairly certain that I'm the only world champion figure skater who can say that—or would want to.

When we had time, Gavin and I explored every inch of the countryside. The rodeo grounds, the river and the garbage dump were prime attractions. We'd salvage odds and ends from the dump, piecing together bikes from discarded frames. Once we built ourselves a high-jump pit. We also found a stack of *Playboy* magazines, which we used to further our education, then hid away. (A porcupine ate them.) Mostly, we'd cart our treasures to a little valley we'd found off the river's backwaters. We also had a private swimming hole and makeshift jungle gym—we shoved tree limbs into holes in the sand cliffs and climbed them to the top. There was a sandbank with a big tree over it, and we'd tie ropes to the tree and swing back and forth, never afraid of falling because of the sand beneath. In winter, we'd ride our bikes on the ice, slipping and sliding up the slope of a frozen beaver dam.

I don't know how all this sounds to you—idyllic or isolated. I didn't think of it either way; to me, it wasn't particularly special. It was all I knew, and it was great. Being on my own out in the country gave me a chance to use my imagination, to build confidence in myself. I didn't know what the word pessimism meant. I had an insatiable curiosity about the world around me, but I never stopped to think about what other kids might be doing in faraway cities. I was too busy racing sticks down the creek, riding bikes and horses, or camping out at Doyle's Pond. That was my world, and it seemed like a pretty good one. I still think so, because I can go back and look at it today. Most of the places where I hung out are still there, virtually intact, ready for me to replay my childhood whenever I want.

I started skating on an outdoor rink when I was three; Dad flooded a small patch of ice in front of the house. When I was six, the Caroline Arena was built. That is where I made my figure-skating debut, in the annual ice carnival. I was in Grade two and I wore a skunk costume.

Dad was one of the volunteers who put the arena up. It was all natural ice, of course—no cooling system or pipes beneath the floors. They must have built it to last, because it's still around, except now it's got fresh plastic on the boards, a larger dressing room and a brand new complex beside it. It also has a brand new name on it—mine!

Some people think that Alberta is a year-round deep-freeze, but that's not true. Chinook winds can send the temperature soaring in February, or bring back Indian Summer overnight, making our winters surprisingly short. You could only bank on four months of skating at the out-side. Every minute counted, so Mom signed me up for both hockey and figure skating, to get the maximum amount of ice time available.

I want you to know I was a half-decent hockey player. I was fast and tricky. I could slide the puck between another player's legs, skate around him and be in the clear on a breakaway before the other team knew what was happening. I'd have played hockey day and night, given the chance. If we heard a rumor that a pond had been cleared, we'd be off like a shot. If there wasn't any ice, we practiced in Gavin's basement. On the team, I played forward and he played defense, but at *his* house, he got to be the shooter

10

and I played goal. At one tournament, he won the trophy for best defenseman and I was named best forward. We'd seen the awards when we walked into the arena and staked our claim on the spot, but we were amazed and really proud of ourselves when we actually won them.

I think that if I'd been bigger, I might have done something in hockey. At five-foot-seven and 145 pounds, I'm not cut out for close encounters with National Hockey League players. I liked it for the same reasons all kids do—the team spirit, the body contact, the sense of immediate accomplishment. You shoot, you score. It's not judged in tenths of a point. I liked it then, and I still do, but I shudder to think of all the things that might have happened to me.

Gavin continued to specialize in defense, and he had a wicked slap shot. Once, when we were in our teens, he sent one flying over the boards. Dad was watching the game. He walked over, bent down and picked up the puck—just as Gavin slammed a second shot that took the exact same path, straight into Dad's chest. Luckily for Dad, he was wearing a down-filled coat. The puck went into it and lodged there. When no puck fell, I remember thinking, "Oh, no! It went right inside my dad!" I was relieved to find that he was alive and kicking, but the shot had cracked one of his ribs just the same.

Hockey wasn't my only sport. I tried everything, and the various teams I played on usually did quite well. Twice we were runners-up at the provincial peewee fastball tournament. We had no uniforms, but lots of guts. Actually, the hockey team was the fastball team was the volleyball team—that's how it works in small towns. I loved track and field, too; I was pretty good at the high jump. I remember that when I was playing hockey, it seemed more important to me than figure skating—but I think in those days whatever sport I was playing instantly became the most important one.

11

Then, when I turned eleven and triumphed at the competition in Lacombe, my coach, Karen McLean, told Mom and Dad that I had real potential, and that if I was going to make anything of figure skating, I should take additional lessons on the artificial ice at Rocky Mountain House, about a half-hour's drive away. I signed up, and Mom and Dad signed away their sleep-in time for the next five years as we began commuting in earnest. Skating lessons took place both before and after school. The family station wagon became a rolling breakfast nook, lunch room and study hall. After my afternoon lesson, there might be a hockey game back in Caroline, so we'd munch on peanut-butter-and-jam sandwiches on the way back.

Later on, when I began to compete more frequently, lessons would be arranged in even more distant towns, where coaching or additional ice time was available. Five-in-the-morning departures and 200-mile round trips were the rule, not an exception, with me stretched out in the cargo area, snoozing through early-morning drives over icy and snow-blown roads.

Karen McLean was the force behind all this. She was the first skating coach I'd met who took the boys seriously, who made me feel that figure skating wasn't only a girl's sport. She had a tremendous amount of energy, and she was a pleasure to be with. She drove a Pontiac Firebird and she drove it hard, always skidding to a stop. She was forever in a rush, but she never failed to notice you on the ice. She made skating make sense, and she made it fun. If she said something, I believed her. So when she said, "You're good, you can jump, you can do a Salchow," I did one. The first double Salchow I ever landed was by accident, just responding to Karen.

It was her idea that I attend a summer figure-skating school, which didn't impress Dad one little bit. It sounded strange to him. Figure skating was fine, he thought, as long as it made for better hockey. It was a real battle talking him into letting me go that week. I went, but I had to use my own savings to pay for it.

Before very long, I started to appear in more and more competitions. Most of them were local ice carnivals. These took place in the spring, as fund-raisers for the upcoming season. Karen also coached a girl named Michelle Pollitt, who was strong enough to lay you flat on your back and cute enough that you'd hang around so she'd hit you again. We trained together at Rocky Mountain House and wound up traveling the province together, usually in the back of Mom and Dad's station wagon. Our big number was "The Mickey Mouse Club" theme (but we didn't wear the ears!).

Michelle and I carved out our own little circuit: Eckville, Bashaw, Red Deer and Ponoka. Soon we skated ice dance—the first and only time I ever appeared with a partner. They lavished prizes on us. Our winnings included twenty-five-dollar gift certificates from local department stores (I always got a jack-knife). One of these appearances was in fact an Alberta sectional competition, and counted toward our progress upward through the various age brackets to the divisional level.

We started making progress. We placed fifth in one year's ice dance event in Lethbridge, but came back strongly the next time around to finish first in St. Albert. We won the pre-juvenile dance, and I've got a silver tray to prove it, along with some faded press clippings with my name misspelled "Curt."

Most of the burden of all this long-distance travel fell on Mom and Dad. They didn't have nine-to-five jobs— they didn't bring work home from the office—so they wound up ferrying whole teams of figure skaters and hockey players around the countryside. I always enjoyed it when they drew the short straw. I'd never think, "Oh, shoot, I have to be on my best behavior." I never changed into a different kind of person. If some other parent drove, the kids might say, "Aw, it's such a pain when Mom comes along." I remember thinking, "Why? You see her every day, don't you? What's the big deal?"

In all these competitions, I was out to win. It always seemed to matter to me to be first at things, whether it was hockey, skating or just getting the best seat on the school bus. One year, on my first day of school, my cousin Miles and I walked all the way to the driver's house before dawn to be sure we'd be first on. But our friends from up the road, Alana and Dustin Moberg, had the same idea. When the driver walked out his door, there we were—four junior overachievers, ready to fight tooth and nail for our chosen places on the bus.

I'll never forget the day I met Mike Slipchuk. I was at a competition in Sherwood Park, outside Edmonton, and I must have been eleven or twelve. There I was in the dressing room, trying to wake up because I'd slept all the way to the meet. The door swung open with a crash and in strolled this little guy wearing glasses with Coke-bottle lenses. He had a head of thick, curly hair, a huge grin and braces on his teeth. He was short and spindly. He didn't look all that strong, but he carried so much confidence that he seemed to overflow the room.

"Hello," he said. "I'm Michael Slipchuk, and I can do a Lutz. What can you do?"

My first thought was, "Well, good for you." My second was, "If this character can really do a Lutz, I'm in trouble." My big jump at that time was a double loop. For a little guy, he sure made a big impression on me.

Today, almost fifteen years later, I still see him as that curly-haired kid. We've been through a lot, laughed and cried together. Our careers have sort of twin-tracked, and several times, people have tried to pit us against each other. Once, a reporter asked "Slipper" if we were really friends, despite competing for the same titles. Then, after he'd taken a shot at Slipper, he asked me the same thing. Both of us answered the same. Yes, we're friends. We use each other to further our careers, to push ourselves in training. But the main thing is that both of us have a friend, someone to rely on absolutely.

We talked about the interview afterward and made a sort of pact. We'd stay friends; we'd never let the media throw us. The longer we skated together, the closer we became. I've always had respect for him. He's a leader, not to mention the Canadian team's good-luck charm. He's never won a medal at the Worlds, but he qualified for them four times. And every time he was there with us, a Canadian won the men's singles title—Brian Orser once, and me the last three years. In Paris, out on the ice one day, I felt lost. I looked up in the stands and there was Slipchuk. He understood what I was going through without a word being spoken.

His mom makes great borscht, he has a dog named Snowball, and I hope he'll be my friend for as long as I'm around.

OTHER VOICES:

Neva and Dewey Browning

Dewey: Kurt was easy to raise. We always had a lot of fun with him, from the time he was little.

Because he came along quite a while after his brother and sister, things were maybe a little easier for Kurt. We had more time and more money to put towards his skating. We could tell him to go ahead and do his best, and we'd back him up.

I guess he got started in skating when I made a little rink for him in the front yard. Once he outgrew that, we signed him up for hockey at the rink in Caroline. The idea of getting him into figure skating didn't come up until we looked at the hockey schedule and saw that the kids only got the ice twice a week, with a game on Saturday. Well, you can't learn to play hockey unless you get more time than that. We thought the figure skating might give him more ice time, and make him a better hockey player, so we signed him up for that, too. But at first, all we were thinking about was hockey!

Neva: We spent a lot of time in those days driving Kurt back and forth to practices. Sometimes it would be a hundred miles away. He'd sleep on an eiderdown in the back of the station wagon, then wake up in time to put his skates on and start training. We never had to nag him into it. He's always had that dedication that you need to be a champion. He loved skating from the beginning and he really wanted to do it. And we enjoyed having that time to spend with him.

Dewey: There are a lot of things we tried to teach him. Most of them are just common sense. Be honest. Do unto others as you wish done to you. Keep your word. And we didn't kid around about rules. In our family, no means no, and we stick to it.

Neva: Kurt knows how to work hard, how to stick with a job till it's finished. I think he got that from us. I guess we did a good job bringing him up, because we get letters from fans thanking us for raising such a great son. I'm just glad he hasn't got an arena head—big and empty!

2

"Mr. J."

I was just two years old when the Soviet tanks entered Czechoslovakia. The occupation of Prague was taking place half a world away, a million light years from the Alberta foothills. But if it hadn't happened, I'd never have met Michael Jiranek, "Mr. J."

He and his wife, Renata, escaped by entering a ball-room dancing competition in West Germany and kept on going, resolved to start new lives elsewhere. They applied to immigrate to Canada and chose Calgary over other cities on the list because they liked to ski.

Mr. J. had been a novice figure-skating champion in his teens. When he and Renata got settled in Calgary and used to Canadian affluence—Mrs. J. made him leave the first grocery store they entered, thinking it was reserved for rich people—he started taking courses to complete a mechanical engineering degree and began coaching skaters on the side. Eventually, he and Mrs. J. bought a ranch near Bashaw, about eighty miles from Edmonton. They took out memberships in the Royal Glenora Club to play tennis and socialize. He'd more or less given up coaching, but after his tennis matches, Mr. J. would stand around watching the skaters working out. One day, the club asked whether he'd help with some part-time instruction. He agreed, and shortly after that we happened to meet at a skating seminar. I was thirteen. I felt comfortable approaching him, because he seemed so calm and patient. Besides, he taught jumping, which was all I really wanted to do.

Mr. J. began to give me advice, just on a day-to-day basis. I think he charged $3.25 a quarter-hour. Pretty soon, though, he began to spend more time with me. Mom and Dad would drive me to Ponoka, a halfway point between Caroline and Edmonton. There was a rink there, and we'd converge on it with Michelle Pollitt, whom he began to coach as well. All this was fairly hit-and-miss, and one day, Mr. J. put it to me straight. "If you're serious about skating," he said, "you should move to Edmonton, so you can get the coaching you need every day."

Here we had a problem. I was fifteen by then, and I wanted to finish Grade ten—the first year of senior high—at the Caroline composite school. All its grades were under one roof. I'd spent nine years in that school, and nobody was going to drag me out of it until I went through at least one senior term, which was your chance to boss the rug-rats around. So we started a twelve-month countdown. Actually, this made things a little easier. It was an important decision, and this way everybody had time to do some thinking.

We spent a long time discussing it. Mom and Dad said, "We're behind you 100 percent, but we want you to sit down and think about this. We want you to look us straight in the eye and tell us you're taking it seriously. You have to promise us that." Which I did. It all worked out, but I can see why Mom and Dad were a little bit nervous.

The move also meant that I had to quit hockey once and for all. There wouldn't be anyone to drive me around in Edmonton; I didn't know anything about the hockey system there. I was placing myself in Mr. J.'s hands. Mom and Dad pointed out that I couldn't divide my time and energies. Travel costs alone would be out of the question. Lord knows that the figure skating was expensive enough. Plus they didn't want me to get hurt on a hockey rink. They said, "You can't do both. Make a choice." In fact, the decision wasn't hard to make.

As it turned out, Mr. J. was perfectly right. That year, 1982, I competed in my first Canadian championships. Mom and Dad drove me all the way to Brandon, Manitoba, across the prairie in February. I placed twelfth among thirteen novice men. I asked Mom if I was really as bad as my marks made out. She thought for a minute, and then said, "Yes." The truth hurt, but the truth was that I badly needed help.

That's how, a few months later, after a competition in Lacombe, I tossed my skate bag into the back of Wade's pickup truck. He was to take me to Edmonton, where I'd stay in the apartment he shared with our cousin, Jennifer Grant. We didn't say much as we stood beside the truck. Mom and Dad had told me they'd back me all the way, and we didn't waste time with goodbyes. It wasn't until we started heading up the road that I realized I'd just left home. No one told me it was going to feel like that. I didn't know that was part of the deal.

Neva and Dewey Browning

Neva: We were happy that Kurt was going to work with Michael Jiranek, because he saw things pretty much the way we did. With Michael, yes is yes, and no is no, and do it again is do it again. Some kids thought he was scary, but Kurt had no problem because he was used to that.

Sending Kurt to Edmonton was a tough decision. Not only was he going to move away from home, but he was going into a very different world—from the ranch to the Royal Glenora Club. He was going to be mixing with a moneyed class of people, and we were afraid that he might feel uncomfortable, left out. I guess we worried for nothing, though, because Kurt didn't seem to mind if he had a penny in his pocket.

Dewey: He was responsible about money. He knew we were sending some pretty big cheques—up to $1,000 a month—so he didn't do anything foolish. We made a deal with him. We told him that if he put all his energy into his training and did his job on the ice, we'd handle the rest of it. And that's the way it went. He never gave us a reason to be sorry for showing so much trust in him.

The move to Edmonton was a huge change, a very traumatic time in my life. I was terribly homesick the first few months. I'd find any excuse to pick up the phone. I'd ride a bus home on Friday and reluctantly head back to the city on Sunday. This went on for weeks; I thought it was never going to end.

My cousin Jennifer helped a lot. I didn't know her very well when I arrived, but we quickly became good friends. Wade was working different jobs, and not having a real great time. He'd separated from his wife and didn't have much time for a little brother he hardly knew. But some of the fondest memories I have are of weekends we'd play hockey on an outdoor rink down the street, after I'd stopped rushing back to Caroline on the slightest pretext.

The first few weeks in their apartment were kind of rough and ready. I slept on the floor, until we moved to another unit in the same building that had an extra bedroom. Wade was a good cook, and Jennifer pitched in. She gave me a crash course in urban living—how to use city transit and get from A to B without mishap. Mostly I rode my bike the eight miles from the apartment to the Royal Glenora Club where I skated—cross-training before they invented the term. Jennifer made sure I was up in the morning, which was a chore, because we'd sit up talking far into the night or watching "Star Trek" reruns on TV.

Eventually, Jennifer and I moved into an apartment of our own, to which I always managed to forget my keys. If it was late, I'd play second-story man—third-story, actually—pulling myself up over people's balconies to enter our apartment through the sliding glass doors rather than hit the buzzer and wake Jennifer up. Other than that, I think we made pretty good roommates. We'd have contests to see who could clean the bedrooms best. I'd put on a Supertramp album and we'd go to it. I usually managed to find a wrinkle in her bedspread and declare myself the winner.

My parents had paid for me to join the Glenora, and it became my home away from home. But they were right—I'd walked into a different social world. Six-year-old kids were casually signing for tins of fruit juice. There was none of this, "Mom, can I have twenty-five cents for some licorice?" It was, "Mom, I charged dinner." It was my first contact with wealth. But, since I didn't have any, I didn't worry about it. Nor did any of the other skaters, no matter how well-off their families happened to be. We looked like a clique, but it was shared interests, not social standing, that was our common bond, and I felt completely comfortable there.

Luckily, I already knew many of the skaters from meets in which we'd competed. There was Slipchuk, Joelle Tustin, Andy Klein, Susan Clark, Karen Scherban, Patsy Schmidt, Melodie Clydsdale, Geoff Hauptman, Todd Goshko, Dorene Kindrachuk, Heidi LeRiche, Laura Schultz, Trina and Jaimie Driscoll, Doug Hemmerling and Elizabeth Howartson. All of them were and still are good friends. All of them are talented as hell. Even then, the Glenora was a magnet for skating talent from all over Alberta. Now, of course, it's a magnet for the world, with kids from across Canada, the States, Japan, Denmark, Sweden and Mexico—a regular United Nations. The important thing was, I'd joined a group of people my own age who lived and breathed skating, and we became very close. We worked together on the ice, hung out together off the ice and traveled together up and down the Western skating division.

I'd met Joelle Tustin at a couple of seminars, and now that I was in Edmonton, we had a chance to get to know each other better and we started dating. She had a wonderful family that I kind of adopted as my own, in-town family. I called her parents Mr. and Mrs. T. I could always tell if Mr. T. was watching when I competed because his voice used to boom out over everybody else's, yelling, "Go for it!" In fact, he still does it today. Joelle and her parents became my escape from school and skating, from working out four or five hours daily in practice, then tackling Grade eleven in a strange and very large collegiate. Joelle and I dated for two years, skating together the whole time, and when the time came to split up, we parted friends.

After about a year, I'd learned my way around the city; I was becoming far more independent. Cousin Jennifer and I took separate apartments, and I missed her company. She was one of my most staunch supporters, and it meant so much to me that she was there for both world championships in Halifax and Munich. So, just for the record, thank you, Jennifer, for being there, and for always being you.

It would be impossible to exaggerate Michael Jiranek's influence on my career. Without him, there might not have been a career at all. His fees were another expense my parents had to shoulder—there were never any freebies—but I like to think it was a good investment on everybody's part. (He now has a small interest in Kurt Browning Enterprises Inc.) He charges $52 an hour now—a modest sum, considering his achievements. He coached Lisa Sargeant to her Canadian women's title; he coached the team of Rod and Karyn Garossino; he looks after fifteen up-and-coming novices and juniors at the Glenora. He's always composed, always supportive and wise.

We've been together for twelve years now and I can count our fights on the fingers of one hand. Of course, our relationship has evolved over those years. When we started out, I had a lot to learn—some would say everything. And his English wasn't so good back then. All he said in many of our lessons was, "Do it again. Again. Okay, Salchow." I didn't mind. I had enough energy to light up a small town. I'd jump and jump and jump the whole day long.

Mr. J. never babysat me, like some other coaches I've seen. In fact, he was a bit like my parents. He always gave me a little bit of rope, but never enough to hang myself. He made me responsible for myself, and I think I responded. Some lessons were spent teaching me the facts of life, not Axels and three-turns. He knows about my personal life; I ask his advice quite often. I think he was quite a charmer in

23

his younger days. But he has different effects on other people. Michelle Pollitt was intimidated by him. People either like him and give him hugs or don't talk to him at all.

To be honest, I don't think I always believed in him. When you're sixteen or seventeen, you're going to rebel against someone or something. Mr. J. was the authority figure, and it wasn't always smooth sailing. But one day, I decided that I would give it my best shot and do what he said until I thought it wasn't working. If and when that happened, I'd do something about it. You know the punchline.

I'm still inspired to get on the ice and make sure he knows I'm doing okay—which is odd, in a way. I mean, how many lessons have we had in twelve years? Theoretically, what have I still got to learn from this guy? But we continue. There are days when I skate just for him. I want to skate so well that there's time for laughing and joking, which he's really good at. We laugh at each other; we laugh at ourselves. The more time we spend together, the more flexible our relationship becomes.

One year, at the Canadian championships, we were laughing our heads off about chastity belts. I was in hysterics; I had tears in my eyes. The other skaters were probably convinced I'd lost it. There we were, minutes away from competition, imagining some dippy knight who goes off to the wars with a key in his armor and comes back shouting, "Hi, honey! I'm home!"—only to discover "John Was Here" scratched on the padlock. I forget how we got on the topic, but it seemed absolutely fascinating at the time. So remember—next time you see us on TV, we may not be discussing the finer points of my performance. We may be off on some strange and wonderful tangent.

Mr. J. reads me well. He knows what to say, and when to say it. He knows I listen to him. We have absolute trust in one another. He runs great interference, creating a buffer zone in which I can relax and psych myself up. I believe in him 110 percent. He's the one who makes me go on the ice and do it, the one who makes me tick.

Michael Jiranek

I like coaching. It's a challenge. It's entertainment. I like working with young people. I consider myself lucky to do something I like and get paid for it. I read somewhere that about 3 percent of the population likes what they do, so I'm doing well.

What I do for Kurt has been changing and developing through the years. When we started working together, I just taught him a fifteen-minute lesson, and then another student came. It was a very basic working relationship, as with any other skater. This started when he was thirteen. At that age, you always see some potential. You always hope this is the one who is going to make it. In Kurt's case, he kept getting better and better. Sometimes we were lucky, sometimes we were good, and it worked out well.

I had no real sense that he was going to be a world champion at the beginning. I don't think the possibility crossed my mind for quite a while. I think our goal was to compete just once in international competition. Don't forget, it's not only a matter of talent. A skater must have the support of his family and the right personality to stay with it and take the hard work, take the falls. You have to be gutsy. Otherwise, you fall a few times and that's it. I've seen so many skaters who go to a certain level, and they start falling while attempting more difficult jumps, and the falls would hurt more and they would quit. To continue, you really have to like it.

So many things come into play to make a world champion out of a raw talent. Talent is maybe one of ten important factors. And you will see talent of a similar caliber, if not in every arena, certainly in every big city. The potential may be there, but the other things don't link together.

Now in Kurt's case, living in Caroline, he wasn't getting enough ice time. He was practicing on natural ice in very cold conditions. He was getting limited coaching. There were so many things against him that would have to be changed in order for him to progress. So the first few years, he was just a talented, entertaining skater. He was easy to coach because he was always bouncy, a bubbly personality. Everything was easygoing.

For quite a while, it was an uphill battle. We have in Canada some skaters who were sent to international competitions very early. Many go before they are fifteen. I believe that Tracey Wainman was twelve. Kurt went for the first time when he was nineteen. By that time, 90 percent of skaters quit if they are not really successful. Then we went to St. Gervais and Oberstdorf and Kurt did quite well. A Canadian Figure Skating Association official named Donald Gilchrist, who also sat on the International Skating Union, was there to examine new judges. And he saw Kurt and said, "This guy looks really promising." He said Kurt reminded him of Ronnie Shaver, a very good jumper who skated for Canada at the Olympics some years ago. So Gilchrist talked to some other officials, and from then on I found it much easier for us. Kurt did well in the next international competitions and very well in the next Canadians. So that was a big step from a steady—what shall I call it?— not achieving much.

Our relationship, as I say, has changed. At first, I was the teacher. Then I started to use psychology as well as the technical teaching. Now I am a bit of many things—friend, confidant, teacher still. But I think the biggest thing is that, when it counted, somehow we always came up with something that worked. When Kurt was in trouble, he looked to me, and I came up with a solution. I feel this is my position. When an athlete is successful, it's all his glory. We only start working when things don't go right.

Does every athlete need a coach, an exterior observer? To perform at 90 percent of his ability and higher, I believe so. On a day-to-day basis, since Kurt is now doing very difficult things, he needs a constant tune-up—on the technique, on timing, on positions. It could slip, little by little, and all of a sudden he wouldn't be able to do it. And actually, some things he can do one day, and next day he cannot. So we have to do the tune-up again. Very little is needed to miss it. Almost every day, we go through a warm-up—easy through more difficult jumps. I have to see them, to monitor them, to correct them if necessary.

Some older, more experienced skaters, in shows and so on, do quite well without a coach, but they are far, far away from their top performances. I am talking now, in Kurt's case, about the highest level of competition. Even on the show circuit, we see Brian Boitano, whose manager is also his coach. His manager-coach is there every day. That may be the reason Boitano continues to skate well.

I do other things for Kurt also. I protect him in competition. I know what is detrimental to his performances, what influences I must try to keep him away from. He is very popular, and he is sometimes infringed upon in such a way that he just goes bananas. So we have to do something to calm him down. Sometimes it may be just a little talk, to make him realize that something, some demand, is not important.

I think some element of planning is always there. Mostly it is a reaction to the surroundings, to the situation. In a way, it gives me a boost as well. If everything went smoothly, I would be falling asleep. Maybe I thrive on the pressure myself. I am more alert, trying to make the best of things and turn the situation to our advantage.

I don't think Kurt has had easy wins. I think the most difficult wins on paper were his easiest, and the toughest were the ones where the competition did not do well. We have seen this all along—at last year's Canadians, last year's Skate Canada. He just barely made it through to win. He had to struggle, because he didn't have that push. If it isn't there, Kurt tends not to skate so well. I think he needs it to get going. Kurt skates better if he has a hammer behind him. Most everybody does better when they are challenged by other talented people

---

In 1983, I went back to take another stab at the novice title at the Canadian championships in Montreal. Most of the skaters had never met; we didn't know anything about each other. The dressing room was buzzing with action, until Brian Orser walked in. Dead silence. No one looked up. He was about to skate for his third consecutive senior title, and his reputation preceded him. None of us could speak a word. We looked at him sideways, to see how he laced his skates, and probably made him nervous in the process.

I was in sixth place going into the free-skating final, after decent showings in the compulsory figures and the original program. That morning, I went for breakfast with a bunch of the other skaters, and we started playing "Who's Going To Win?"

"It'll probably be you," I told Darren Kemp, who was looking good in fourth place. "I'm sixth. I'm out of it."

Later on, getting ready to head for the rink, I was standing in the hotel hallway with my skate bag when Rod Garossino, Mr. J.'s former student, walked by.

"I was just talking to Mr. J., and he says you're going to win," Garossino said. "Good luck."

"No, no," I said. "I'm in sixth. I can't possibly win."

"Well, he said you could," Garossino insisted. "I'll be rooting for you."

I didn't have a clue what was going on, but I found Coach J. in a hurry. "What's this about me being able to win?" I asked.

"You can win," he said. "Don't make any mistakes, don't leave anything out, and you'll win."

"Okay," I said. Then I went out and won the thing.

After I'd skated, I was led into the media center, a hive of unaccustomed activity. Cameras were rolling, banks of computers were tabulating scores, reporters were busily filing stories, and people I'd seen only on television— including Johnny Esaw, the CTV executive who did so much to promote the popularity of figure skating—were standing close enough to touch. It was a heady atmosphere for a wide-eyed teenager. In a few years, it would be commonplace, but then it seemed like a cross between a three-ring circus and a zoo.

A guide plopped me down in front of Donald Jackson— that took my breath away. Jackson was the first Canadian to win the world title, in 1962; the first man to land a triple Lutz in competition (a feat that wouldn't be duplicated at the world level for a dozen years); an inspiration to everyone who's ever laced up a pair of skates. Naturally, I thought he'd dropped by specially to congratulate me on my performance. I didn't grasp that he was filing stories to a Toronto newspaper. I also didn't know I'd won the gold medal, having fled the rink before the scores were posted.

"How does it feel to be Canadian novice champion?" Jackson asked.

For a second, I thought he was crazy. Then *I* went crazy, dancing the "Dance of Joy" in front of him, not making terribly much sense. "Wow, I won!" I shouted. "Ohmigod, I won!" And so on, for what must have seemed to Jackson an eternity. He was sitting there, quite probably thinking, "I don't believe this kid. He doesn't know I'm interviewing him. He doesn't know he's won. Here we have a definite credit to the sport. How did he make it on the plane unaided?" So that's how I met Donald Jackson, won a medal I didn't think I had a chance of winning and learned to trust Mr. J.'s advice forever.

Michael Jiranek

I remember this incident quite well. I had met Rod Garossino at the hotel. I wasn't coaching him that year; he had moved from Calgary to Toronto. He asked me who I had brought to the competition. I told him that I had a novice man. Garossino said, "Is he any good?" "Yes," I said, "he's going to win."

I did not arrange this meeting. That is, I did not tell Garossino that Kurt would win, knowing that Rod would in turn tell Kurt. But obviously, I had not told Kurt about his chances. Why not? I don't think you can be too positive sometimes. It was probably a good coincidence that my belief bounced off another person. If I had gone straight to Kurt at the outset and said, "You do this and this, and you will win," he'd just have looked at me and said, "Well, yes, and I'm the President of the United States." That's an approach you would expect from a coach who was overdoing things.

For a skater, a very young skater, who was trying hard, and who was, after the first part of the competition, sixth, it's hard to change his mind. It doesn't work that way. Later, yes. At that time, no. So it was merely a fortunate coincidence. I was surprised when Kurt came and asked me about it. At that point, I had to be direct; I couldn't deny what he'd already been told. Still, you will agree, it worked out reasonably well.

Winning the novice championships was all the more special because Marvin Trimble, Gavin's cousin and a buddy from the Caroline Figure Skating Club, was there to see it. The previous summer, we'd sat around a campfire back home, and he'd told me that, if I made it to a national competition again after my less than auspicious debut in Brandon, he'd go to watch me win. I had no idea he'd actually made it. I arrived in Montreal, and Mom told me he was there. As it turned out, I'm very glad he was, because it was thanks to him that I made it back home.

Apparently, Mr. J. and Marvin were the only people who believed I had a chance at a medal. Marvin had booked his return flight for late Sunday night so that he could watch the champions perform in a post-awards exhibition. All the Alberta skaters and their families were booked out Sunday morning, because the provincial skating association hadn't counted on us winning anything. I wanted badly to appear in the gala, but to alter my ticket cost $325. Mom and Dad flew in the morning as planned, leaving me a credit card to pay for my re-booked seat on the evening flight. I skated in the exhibition, wishing they were there, but happy that Marvin could share in my first-ever gold medal at the Canadians.

At the airport that night, however, the ticket clerk refused to accept the credit card shoved at her by an obvious minor without a word of authorization.

"I'm in trouble," I said to Marvin. "No problem," he assured me. "I've got $325." I was flabbergasted. "You carry that kind of money with you all the time?" "Well," he said, "maybe not all the time, but I usually have a little extra hidden away."

With that, he bent over, pulled off a running shoe and removed a wad of bills from underneath the insole. It had poured rain that day, with the result that both Marvin's feet and the money were soaking wet. Water dripped sadly from a stack of twenties and tens, which he handed to the astonished ticket clerk. She took the soggy bills into a back room. Marvin had five dollars change due, and I swear she ran it underneath a tap. She handed it to him with a grim smile and wished him an extra-nice day. You'll be happy to know that Marvin was reimbursed by the skating association when we landed. I must ask him sometime if he still carries money in his shoes.

And so much for my first taste of victory. In the weeks and months that followed, I'm sorry to say that my ego gained the upper hand. I was one hotshot skater. I worked on new programs and learned new jumps for the 1983-84 season with a very cocky attitude. This is usually a recipe for disaster, and disasters seem to befall me in groups of three and four.

In January of 1984, on the eve of my departure for the divisional qualifying competition in Calgary, I was driving "the Ark," a fourth-hand 1974 Buick Le Sabre, when I mistakenly got into the wrong lane and was hit by another driver. The impact threw me to the floor on the passenger side, covered with broken glass. I managed to get my hand on the brake pedal, stopped the car and crawled out, unhurt but badly shaken up. The worst part of it was the phone call to Caroline that night. Mom and Dad had given me the car.

Somehow this near-miss sent me skidding out of contention at the divisionals in January 1984. I placed seventh, and failed to advance to the junior event at the Canadian championships in Regina, Saskatchewan. I felt as if I'd flunked a year in school, and my teacher was not amused. That night, Mr. J. gave me a Grade-A tongue-lashing, maybe the loudest I've ever had. Worse yet, I knew I deserved it.

At the time, I felt as if the sky had fallen. In retrospect, though, I think that my terrible showing was a valuable lesson, my first rude and much-needed shock. Seven years later, as I walked out of the Olympic Hall in Munich, second to Viktor Petrenko following the original program and needing a superior performance in the free skate to win my third world title, I'd think back on the low points of my career, the times I'd skated myself into a deep and murky hole. The Calgary divisionals were first on the list, but would not be the last.

3

A FULL-TIME JOB CALLED FIGURE SKATING

Let me tell you what I thought I'd be doing in 1984. I honestly thought I'd be heading for the Winter Olympics in Sarajevo, Yugoslavia. I remember this well, because I put it on paper at one of the CFSA's regional seminars. These were extremely valuable get-togethers organized by the association to monitor coaching and make sure that fresh talent found its way onto the national team. All the participants were asked to write down their goals and aspirations for the future, and I surprised Barbara Graham, the CFSA's technical coordinator, by announcing that I was going to be in the spotlight at Sarajevo. Graham pointed out that this was perhaps a touch over-ambitious, that the 1988 Olympics in Calgary were a somewhat more realistic goal. So they were—but I think that's when Graham and the CFSA realized that I was determined to go all the way. She has since retired, and we will all miss her.

I continued to attend the seminars. At a regional meet in Vancouver, later in 1984, I met Tracey Wainman, who'd won the Canadian women's senior title three years earlier. Compulsory figures were one of her many strong points; she taught me a lot in one short week. At the same time, I met Brian Power, the choreographer who'd be responsible for my programs at the Munich Worlds.

The national seminars were usually held in London, Ontario, and they were a joy. I kissed Nathalie Sasseville in an elevator (those were the days when one kiss could make or break a summer), Norm Proft and I saw the Beach Boys in concert, and I attended plays at Stratford's Shakespeare Festival. The seminars were a cross between summer camp and Marine Corps basic training. We were untried kids, struggling to impress the coaches and knocking ourselves out to attract attention. We'd skate at the University of Western Ontario Arena, where one night I attempted to high-jump a parking lot barrier gate. Moral: never take off from a patch of pavement that's slick with motor oil. I lost my footing and grabbed the gate, which promptly snapped in two. After a good old-fashioned third-degree at the security guard's office, we settled on a twenty-five-dollar repair bill. I had all of twenty-five cents in my pocket, so I fast-talked the guard into letting me get a cheque from my dorm. When I got back and wrote it out, he ripped it up. He had a cousin who taught skating in Alberta; he figured that westerners ought to stick together.

I worked hard in London, determined to rebound from my failure in Calgary. My first chance to compete again came in August 1984, when Alberta sent a contingent to the Arctic Blades competition in Los Angeles. The idea behind Arctic Blades was to expose promising skaters to a wider range of competition, people we'd never seen before, especially the "Intimidating Americans." We quickly realized that their level of training was higher than ours. Alberta sent about ten skaters each year. If they were lucky, one or two would return with medals of some description. Competitions like Arctic Blades don't change anyone's standing back home. They are just confidence-builders; they improve your image in the eyes of the judges and enhance your reputation and confidence. It seems to be working; each year our team does a bit better than the year before.

I remember stepping onto the practice rink, my first glimpse of the international circuit. It looked more like an anthill, swarming with skaters of every age. That year, I finished fifth at the junior level, landing a triple loop for the first time in competition, and went home feeling pleased with myself.

That was the autumn that I decided to ease the financial pressure by taking a waiter's job. I went to school in the morning, worked an afternoon shift and skated all evening long. Then, if I felt up to it, I did my homework. Both school and skating began to suffer almost immediately. Six months later, I abandoned the experiment. I must admit, though, that it was interesting. Everybody should be a waiter at least once. (O.K., who ordered the Mexican Pizza?)

Training that fall and winter went well, until I cut my foot during the takeoff for a Lutz jump—the beginning of an unbroken bad-luck streak with the Lutz that seemed to last forever. It had been a long practice, and I'd missed the Lutz on my last eight or nine tries. Mr. J. knew how tired I was, so he left me with strict instructions: No more jumps that day. What could I do, then, when Mrs. Rosemary Marks asked to see the Lutz one more time? I knew that I shouldn't do it, but she was an important judge, and I didn't feel I could say no. It turned out to be a very bad idea. During the takeoff, my left foot shot back and the tail end of the blade pierced my right boot and went straight into my foot. I didn't realize how bad it was until I pulled off my boot and found the sock drenched with blood. Five stitches later, the doctor ordered me to take ten days off. After that, just warming up for a Lutz made my heart race like crazy. It was years before I really mastered my feelings and was able to put the Lutz back in my programs.

By January the cut had barely healed, and it was time for the 1985 divisionals in Moose Jaw, Saskatchewan. Our team had adopted the TV character Gumby as a mascot, and Val Lloyd showed up with a five-foot-tall replica. (She was a teammate and a good seamstress!) The British Columbia skaters retaliated with posters reading: "Gumby's Body Is Long and Slender / But When B.C. Gets Him, He's In The Blender." They kidnapped our giant friend, but we managed to secure his release. A few weeks later, he showed up at the Canadian championships in Moncton, New Brunswick, where my program won me the junior title. I hit a double-toe/triple-toe combination, beating out my closest rival, Matthew Hall. As I took my bow, Gumby came sailing onto the ice, tossed from the stands by an enthusiastic cheering section. I'm pretty sure that set the record for the largest object ever thrown on ice after a figure-skating performance (although maybe I shouldn't say that—it might inspire people to bigger and better unguided missiles in the future).

I turned nineteen in June 1985 and received the best birthday present I could have wished for—an invitation from the CFSA to skate on the international circuit. My first performance was at the Coup d'Excellence in Montreal, where Christopher Bowman of the United States won and I placed a respectable fifth. Chris was in top form. After falling on a triple Lutz and catching his blade in some decorations at the end of the rink, he recovered by doing the Lutz again in the last ten seconds of the free-skating final. He left a lasting impression—but so did Christine Hough, who was skating pairs with Doug Ladret. Everyone called her Tuffy, and I liked her the first time I saw her. Pretty soon the feeling grew, and we began to date. Montreal was my first international competition, my first triple Lutz in competition and my first taste of what my life would be like for the next seven years.

In August 1985, I flew to Europe for the first time, for competitions in St. Gervais, France and Oberstdorf, West Germany. We landed in Paris, bused to St. Gervais, in the shadow of Mont Blanc, and checked into the Maison Blanche, a small hotel where the Canadian teams made a habit of staying. The thing I remember most is that the entire town was preparing a gigantic vat of French onion soup, the largest ever made, in hopes of breaking a world record. It sat in the town square, in a cauldron maybe five feet high and seven feet across.

This was the first time I'd ever been overseas. Europe gave me the feeling of having existed forever. I truly understand how young my own country is in comparison. I decided that everything I'd heard about the French was true and retreated to my hotel room. Tradition held that all the skaters sign their names on the bottoms of the dresser drawers in the upstairs bedrooms, so we spent the evening reading messages left by team members in previous years. It was like opening a time capsule.

I'm glad to say that this time I skated well. I won the free-skating final, finishing second overall behind Doug Mattis, the U.S. junior champion. Tuffy and Doug Ladret won the pairs title, which gave us reason to celebrate on the final night before hopping a bus to Geneva, then a train to Oberstdorf, just north of the Austrian border. It was aboard that train that I ran afoul of the "Soviet Hordes."

You have to realize that I had led a fairly sheltered life—being on a train was not an everyday experience. I'd hardly ever seen a Russian before, but, like all skaters, I thought I knew all about them. They were the next best thing to invincible. They arrived, and you lost; it was as simple as that. In those days, relatively few of them spoke much English, so we weren't exactly chattering away together as the train rolled along, then stopped, in the middle of the night and (as far as I could see) the middle of nowhere. After a while, several people got off and began wandering around. For some reason I got it into my head that everyone had to leave the train immediately. I suppose I'd convinced myself that it was a border crossing. In any case, I thought I'd do my bit to further cordial relations with the Communist bloc.

The Soviet skaters were sound asleep in their compartment, like sensible people. I pounded on their door, which opened to reveal a scene rather like a den, crammed with sleepy Soviet bears. I made encouraging and imperative noises; I paraded out all the sign language I could think of. Groggily and grudgingly, the Russians followed me off the train and milled disconsolately around the platform.

Slowly, it began to dawn on me that not everybody was getting off. Worse yet, it began to dawn on the Russians, too. There was only one thing to do, and I did it. I crept back to my seat and tried to make myself invisible. No such luck. The Soviet contingent filed by, each one giving me the filthiest look he could muster. That night, international relations took a definite turn for the worse.

It was a relief to arrive in Oberstdorf, but that relief was short-lived. Nearby was a gorge with a beautiful waterfall; we hiked out to admire it one morning. By the time I'd finished skating, I felt as if I'd been swept over the precipice. A belly-flop on the first jump of my free skate knocked the wind out of me and knocked me way down in the standings. In spite of the fact that this competition was basically a rerun of the first, I dropped all the way from second at St. Gervais to ninth, well behind the leader, Richard Zander of West Germany. Mr. J. refrained from reading me the riot act, but he was getting tired of my on-again, off-again performances.

In October 1985 I competed at the Skate America competition in St. Paul, Minnesota, finishing eighth overall. Poland's Jozef Sabovcik won the gold medal, with Brian Boitano of the United States second, Viktor Petrenko third and Christopher Bowman fourth. It was the toughest field I'd encountered to that point. I blew my first figure in the compulsories, placing twelfth and last. I was a mammoth five inches out on one of the turns and felt bitterly disappointed by my imprecision.

During the free skate I hurt my back, but I didn't know what the problem was. The team doctors poked and prodded but for some reason failed to suggest an X-ray. I skated on, despite mounting discomfort. I was younger then; I wouldn't be so cavalier today.

After the Christmas break, I attended the 1986 divisional competition in Delta, British Columbia, where I had no trouble advancing to the Canadian championships in North Bay, Ontario that February. This was my first opportunity to compete at the senior level, which meant I was skating against Orser.

I can remember standing with the rest of the group looking out to the clean ice and TV lights before the original program. The men's event was always exciting, and I was about to see it from the inside out this time! The fellow beside me had a terrific outfit, with what looked like real leather on the top. Without thinking, I reached out to touch it—sure enough, it was real leather. You can imagine the funny look on Brian Orser's face as he looked around to see who was tugging on his sleeve twenty seconds before his warm-up. "Real leather?" I asked. "Yup," he said. Then he smiled and went back to his own thoughts. I guess my curiosity gets the better of me sometimes. Right at that moment, I felt as if I was back in the dressing room in Montreal when I was a novice!

Orser retained his title with ease, followed by Neil Paterson and Jaimee Eggleton; Kevin Parker was fourth, and I came fifth.

The big surprise that week was Tracey Wainman, who'd been out of competition for more than two years but fought back to regain the women's title from Elizabeth Manley. The big disappointment was that my back was killing me. I had a session with one doctor, who said, "Do you mind if I try acupuncture?" Meanwhile, he'd been inserting the needles; I hadn't felt a thing. But whatever he did achieved no lasting good. And no wonder. When I got back to Edmonton, I headed straight for the University of Alberta Hospital. This time, an X-ray revealed a hairline fracture of my fourth lumbar, and I was ordered off the ice for two long months.

I used this enforced downtime to take stock of my situation, and came to a decision. Basically, I felt I had to call a halt to school. Although I'd completed Grade twelve in Edmonton, I never really felt a part of the high school I attended, because I was so seldom there.

At one point, I'd thought vaguely of becoming an architect. I liked drawing, and I liked the idea of creating something tangible. I took drafting classes and showed at least some promise. I'm good with my hands—I still produce leatherwork as a hobby—and I think I have a half-decent visual sense. The trouble was, I couldn't get my assignments in on time. This trouble persisted when I went on to Alberta College. It was like a community college, with lots of mature students and people busy juggling classes and jobs. I took biology, mathematics and physics courses, but faded out of the school scene after a couple of years, never to return.

Why did I quit? Because I had a full-time job called figure skating. It was an easy decision. I didn't choose skating; it chose me. Most of my classmates were feeling their way, uncertain where they were going. What I was born to do was right in front of me. I'd been knee-deep in it, devoting most of my energies to it, ever since I'd moved from Caroline to Edmonton. Now I'd reached a critical point, where every hour of lost ice time was reflected in my training. I didn't know if I had a long-term future in skating; I wasn't thinking in terms of world championships. But I was fairly certain that, if I applied myself, I could make it as far as the Canadian championships after Orser hung up his skates. This seemed a reasonable, attainable goal, so I buckled down to achieve it.

My first step was to finish among the top three seniors in Canada, to win a spot on the team that would be sent to the Worlds in Cincinnati, Ohio, in March 1987. In August 1986, I returned to St. Gervais, where I won the silver medal, landing—for the first time—both a triple Lutz and a triple flip in the same program. I took a bronze a few days later at Oberstdorf; I would have scored even higher but I fell on one of my landings. Vitalij Egorov of the Soviet Union won the gold, and that was the last I ever heard of him. A lot of skaters have disappeared from the world standings as I've worked my way up.

Oberstdorf marked a turning point. It was the first time I tried a quadruple toe-loop in public. It was a disaster; the landing went every which way but right. It didn't count, because it took place during the post-competition gala, and just as well. It was a far cry from the quads I'd been landing consistently in practice sessions back at the Royal Glenora. (The first one I'd completed took place late at night. Rae Del Rusnak and I were the only people on the ice, and neither of us could believe I'd actually done it.) The rest of my programs were coming together nicely, thanks to Sandra Bezic, the Toronto choreographer who was of great help in improving my free-skating style.

My next stop was Japan, in November, for the NHK Trophy competition, sponsored by the NHK television network. It's strictly for exposure and experience; there's no prize money involved. But, as with any international competition, more than prestige is on the line. All these competitions count for something. The judges remember your placement; it colors their expectations. You can look forward to an easier time at subsequent matches if you demonstrate that you're making progress throughout the season. By implanting that thought, you edge a little closer to the podium.

Let me tell you about Japan. By this time, I'd seen a bit more of the world. In fact, I was getting rather used to it—the globe-trotting traveler!—but Japan just stopped me in my tracks. Alberta's wide-open spaces hadn't prepared me for Tokyo's subway pushers, who shove passengers onto the cars like so many sardines. I couldn't fathom it; I just stood and gaped. The supermarkets had teams of young women who greeted you when you came in, and others who thanked you on the way out. There were armies of street-sweepers, some of whom had twig brooms, like the wicked witch. There were machines that both painted lines on the pavement and blew the paint dry as it went along, so that a lane would be closed only for a minute or so; none of this business with flagmen and pylons. There wasn't time; there wasn't space. Even the parking lots were unlike anything I'd ever seen. You drove inside and onto a sort of turntable, which revolved to point your car at a certain angle. Then it was driven by the attendant into a huge hanging basket, which disappeared upward, taking your car with it. The whole place was filled with cars, swaying above you in these baskets, like bats in a cave. This eliminated the need for access ramps. I felt like the Shrinking Man, trapped inside an automated sandwich-vending machine. (Which reminds me—I also tried sushi for the first time in my life. I didn't mind the whitefish, but a slice of octopus came complete with suction cup, which stuck to the side of my bowl. I decided not to press my luck any further.)

At the rink, I looked around and weighed my chances. Alexandr Fadeev of the Soviet Union, the 1985 world champion, was gliding confidently to and fro. No way I was going to get past him. Finally, I decided that at least I could count on beating Angelo D'Agostino, from the United States. For some reason, he didn't impress me that day, and I put him out of my mind. Naturally, he won the gold with a tremendous skate. Fadeev missed two elements in his original program, landing him firmly in last place, after which he pulled out of the free skate. Moral: never take anyone for granted. Ever since that day, when I walk into an arena, there aren't any assumptions cluttering up my mind. Everyone starts off equal; everyone is equally dangerous and deserving of respect.

I had a day or so to spare, and spent the time seeing more of the city, zooming around on my Ultrawheels skates, which strangely enough—the Japanese seem to be first with everything else—attracted a lot of attention. So did my teammate, Patricia Schmidt, who has flowing blond hair. So did Midori Ito; the diminutive female star has a following in Japan that Wayne Gretzky might envy. I was surprised at skating's widespread popularity. The Japanese audiences are very attentive and appreciative, very sophisticated, but capable of rabid loyalties. Midori can't go anywhere without being mobbed by well-wishers. Not surprisingly, she gets anxious and nervous when she's surrounded by people pulling and pushing at her. Sometimes, when we were on tour in Europe, I would help her escape from the arena after a gala show. It was fun playing bodyguard for her, and she would be so happy she'd laugh and bounce up and down as soon as she was safely on our bus.

Three more events stick in my mind. First was the daring rescue of Fred the Fish. Outside our hotel there were two ponds filled with goldfish. One pond was much smaller than the other and contained a single, very lonesome fish. We talked to him every night; he became our mascot away from home. When the competition ended, we got a garbage pail, scooped Fred out of the water and transferred him to the pool containing all his friends. We felt sure we'd saved his life and done wonders for his social standing.

Second was my first sight of Katarina Witt, the East German ice princess who'd lost her world title to Debbie Thomas of the U.S. the previous spring. Witt was fond of showing up in a practice outfit that looked more like lingerie, which served to keep everyone awake.

Third was my tragic descent into a career of crime. Let me put this as delicately as possible. Japanese hotels provide their guests with marvelous cotton robes. It had become traditional for NHK contestants to obtain a lifetime supply, which they give to friends and family. The world is full of skaters who've never set foot in Japan but nonetheless luxuriate in these gowns. Merely to uphold the tradition, I liberated some to take home, but Scott Chalmers went too far. His suitcase looked as if it had been force-fed clothing for months. "What have we here?" demanded the customs man. "I'm not opening that bag," said Scott. "Go ahead, if you want. But I'm warning you—you do so at your own risk." No inspector worth his salt is going to pass up that sort of challenge. The pressure-packed bag was cautiously unzipped and showed signs of certain explosion. The customs officer thought again and decided to let Scott go through. That was a close one! Let the record show that while I made skaters and friends happy with my actions, it had just the opposite effect on my mother. She was a bit angry that I'd stolen them—so I didn't give her one!

It just occurred to me that, in the midst of all these stories, I've perhaps been making too many assumptions. I hope I haven't confused anybody by throwing around the names of various jumps, by not explaining in detail the moves that go into my skating. If you've followed the sport, you probably know what I'm talking about; you can see it in your mind's eye. The trouble is, these things are second nature to me. If I were standing in your living room, I could go through the motions. To describe them in words is difficult, something I've never had to do before. But here goes.

Just as a golfer doesn't have to murder the ball to get it down the fairway, a skater who knows how to jump doesn't have to jump hard. When I do a triple toe-loop, I'm not heaving my body into the air. It's all in the technique.

When I plant my toe-pick and push into a jump, my balance changes as I lift into the air. Everything must happen in the proper sequence, properly timed. If you can accomplish that, it takes surprisingly little energy. That's why I'm capable of executing, say, a triple-triple combo at the very end of a demanding program. I'm tired, but I still have a reserve of mental strength. I can summon up the necessary concentration, shake off the fatigue and avoid the temptation to try too hard, which usually dooms the attempt.

And now, to work. There are two basic types of jump: those involving takeoff from the edge of the skate blade (Axel, Salchow and loop) and the toe (Lutz, toe and flip). Most skaters rotate counter-clockwise in midair, with the left leg crossed over the right, the feet together and the legs straight. Most takeoffs are from the left foot, most landings on the right. The hands are clenched in front of the chest with elbows down and slightly extended. The head usually faces over the left shoulder. All jumps look pretty much alike to the casual observer—and sometimes, to the trained eye. But these are some of the distinguishing features to watch for.

The Axel, named for Axel Paulsen (who introduced it way back in the 1880s), is the only jump that you enter traveling forward. It involves an extra half-rotation in midair, so a triple Axel is actually three and a half turns. You take off from the front part of the left outside blade edge and land on the right outside edge. Axels are difficult jumps to master. The first time I landed a double, I was fourteen, at a summer skating school in Calgary. I'd been working on it all week, and had a bruised tailbone to show for my pains.

Now I have fun with Axels, but I treat them with respect. My takeoff looks as if I'm about to try for a basketball slam-dunk; my right leg and both arms are thrown very high. Then I spin, while traveling fifteen feet across the ice. The right foot takes a lot of punishment from the force of the landing. Sometimes I lose control and jump too hard or too high. I can feel it when I come down; the shock wave goes shooting up into my knee. Sometimes I'm up too long and can't ride out the curve I've sketched in my mind. This means trouble. My foot lands inside the curve, but my body keeps going toward the outside. Torque seizes my knee. This is the way most knee injuries occur. Still, the Axel is one of my favorite jumps because of its power. You can't go to Worlds with a garden-variety triple Axel. You've got to get out and sell it, make it better than anyone else's. It's the king of jumps.

The Salchow is named for Ulrich Salchow, who was world champion ten times between 1900 and 1911. It consists of a takeoff from the left back inside edge, as many revolutions as you think you can get away with and a landing on the right back outside edge. It's similar to the Axel in that both feature left-footed takeoffs and right-footed landings. But you enter it moving backward which (curiously enough) makes it easier to learn.

The Lutz is a relative latecomer, named for Alfred Lutz, who unveiled it in the 1930s. Here you take off from the left back outside edge while digging in with the right toe, rotate counter-clockwise and land on the right back outside edge. The Lutz requires a lot of momentum. You have to transfer all your weight to the right toe before you throw the left leg up, then start turning to the left. This is not the natural thing to do; you feel as if unseen hands are holding you back. The only difference between a Lutz and a flip is that, with the latter, you're on the inside edge.

The Lutz and I did not agree for quite a while. I wasn't shifting my weight quickly enough, and was

47

always off-balance. I've told you about my accident on the takeoff in 1985. I've had not one, but three such accidents, for a total of fifteen stitches. Oddly enough, I had a great Lutz as a junior, but after my accidents I wanted no part of it. I could do all the other jumps in my sleep, or visualize them before I jumped. I look forward to doing it now, but the Lutz and I were enemies for a long time.

The toe-loop (there ought to be a Norwegian named Loop, but there isn't) involves a takeoff from the right back outside edge while digging in the left toe, as many revolutions as you're up for and a landing on the same edge. Actually, the toe-loop is attributed to Werner Rittberger, who skated in the early 1900s. Since for a while I was avoiding not one but two jumps—the Axel and the Lutz— the toe-loop seemed a blessing, and comparatively easy on my back. The tricky parts are controlling momentum on the takeoff blade and turning immediately off the toe. I had such a good time with triple toe-loops that I decided to take the next logical turn!—but that's another story.

Before we leave the jumps, I'd like to lay claim to a complete latecomer—"the waxel." Someday it will be recognized in competition. The waxel starts with a botched takeoff. Think of a pole vaulter who doesn't plant his pole. It is is a ceiling-to-ice jump. That is, you find yourself in mid-air, trying to keep your head straight and wondering how (if at all) you're going to come down. But your head is going up and down like a yo-yo—ceiling-to-ice, ceiling-to-ice. This does not impart a feeling of confidence. You look like a boat, hydroplaning out of the water. In September 1990 I executed a perfect "waxel." I came down with my hands out in front of me to cushion my fall, having figured out that I was going to go forward on my face, not back on my skull. I'd forgotten that ice is a slippery substance. My hands kept going, and I put my teeth through my upper lip. It was a very neat, almost surgical opening, about the size of a dime. Several stitches later, I was back in business.

But be alert for "waxels" the next time you're watching our otherwise faultless performances on TV.

Those are the building blocks. Here's what you have to do with them. The original program (formerly the short) is a series of required jumps, footwork and spins. In the free skate (formerly the long program) you can do anything you please—well, almost! Both programs are marked out of 6.0, for both technique and artistic impression. Mandatory elements for the original program change from year to year, just to keep us on our toes. Here, for example, is what we had to do in 1990: one double Axel; one triple jump of any description, preceded by connecting steps and/or comparable movements; a combination consisting of a double-triple or two triples; one flying jump spin; one spin with at least two changes of foot and one change of position; one spin combination with a change of foot and at least two changes of position; and two different step sequences.

There are only a few restrictions in the free-skating program. Try to stay with me now. There are six basic triples, and you are basically allowed to perform each of these only once. You can choose two of them to duplicate, as long as the second one is in combination with another double or triple jump. So, after you tally this up, you see that the skater can attempt only eight triples in one four-and-a-half-minute skate. (Only?) This is a good rule, since it prevents a skater from making his whole routine out of ten triple toe-loops—very boring! Also, it gives the skater a chance to show that he can perform all six different triples. If you don't stick to this rule, you risk a deduction in your mark, just as in the original program.

Aren't you glad there won't be questions? Aren't you doubly glad you aren't a judge, who has to keep track of all this and make sure I execute it flawlessly, marking me down in tenths of a point if I don't?

And now, a word about figures. This is sort of ancient history because they've been eliminated from world

49

competition, but they loomed large when I was making my way up. They're more than a building block, they're the very basis of competitive skating.

A big reason they've been done away with is that people hate to watch them. They don't make for pulse-quickening TV. The description you usually hear is "Like watching paint dry." Now that they're gone, I miss them. Let me tell you just a bit about them.

Peter Jensen, the sports psychologist attached to the CFSA, who was always around with his wisdom and advice, used to help me with my figures, and I needed all the help I could muster. He suggested that I approach them by imagining I was on a diving board, ready to take the plunge. The ice was perfectly clean. There'd be no music; I had to initiate the first movement myself. It was like being a writer, staring at a blank sheet of paper, or an artist, hesitating before making the first brush stroke on a canvas. This is unsettling and intimidating. So are the judges, who watch the procedure with a combination of boredom and intense interest.

Figures take years to master. They're technically difficult. They're very precise, very academic, compared with the flamboyant jumps and spins. As you move along (always on one foot only) through the circles, loops, figure-eights and curves, you should leave a track on the ice. When you turn on the circle, you should leave a mark in the shape of a little mountain, a tiny, perfect peak. This means that you're traveling on one edge of the skate blade. Then you switch edges, entering on one, leaving on the other. Then you do the whole thing over again. The second track should be right on top of the first. At the world level, if they're more than one or two finger-widths apart, you're giving the judges a reason to deduct marks. This is called tracing the figure.

I had to learn how to do these. Some skaters use a scribe, like a giant protractor, to help them trace the initial figure. Actually, I got to the point where my first tracings went fairly well, but my second and third tracings were where I lost most of my marks, and sometimes almost my lunch! When I came around to retrace them, I felt dizzy, as if I were balanced on a tightrope wire.

Mr. J. was a great believer in figures. He absolutely loved them. I think that he himself must have been very good at them when he was skating. It frustrated him that I couldn't do them, and he was never in a better mood than when I did them well. I seemed to have no talent for, or interest in, the figures. So they became even more rewarding for Mr. J. My jumps were there, inside of me, ready to be brought out, refined and improved. I had that talent. But the figures were something I had to learn—there was no getting around them—and they were something for which I truly needed his help. He's unhappy that they're gone from the world scene.

Figures used to count for an absurd percentage of your final marks. Way back when, I think it was 60 percent, then 50 percent, then 30 percent and finally 20 percent. That's why, by the way, I could score poorly in figures and still achieve a good final placement by racking up points in the original and free-skating programs.

Anyway, you might think—in your role as imaginary judge—that figures were at least easy to evaluate. You couldn't go wrong. They weren't subjective. You couldn't possibly argue about them. They were right there, for everyone to see. Wrong. Christopher Bowman's coach called them the last bastion of manipulation. There used to be a ridiculous discrepancy in the judges' marks. Let me give you an example. At the world championships in Paris, the British judge placed me first in figures. The Canadian judge thought I was second. The Australian, third. The West German, fourth. The Finnish, fifth. Bulgaria, the Soviet Union and Switzerland placed me sixth, and Hungary put me eighth. This is obviously not a logical process.

It led Toller Cranston, when he'd finished his last figure, to throw his skates off a bridge.

It was in fact quite easy to psych the judges out. If you looked as if you were under control, they wouldn't suspect mistakes. If not, they'd make a beeline for a certain spot and say, "Aha! He's got a flat!" That's what happens when you're on both edges of the blade at once and you leave two little tracks instead of one. Despite all this, I was actually enjoying figures near the end. I grew to appreciate them. And finally—despite what everybody thinks—I mastered them, just when the International Skating Union pulled the plug. When I came second in compulsory figures at Halifax, it represented my greatest improvement in any aspect of skating. I'm proud to say that I'm the only skater to have won the Worlds both with figures and without.

Part of my success with figures in the last years came from my late-night sessions. Not all the time, but when the mood hit me, I would go down to the Royal Glenora at about 11:00 at night. If the ice needed flooding, I drove the Zamboni myself, making my own ice. Then, with my favorite music on, I would practice my figures all alone. Sometimes for three or four hours my life would slow right down, almost like meditation. After I was finished, I always took ten minutes to go around the whole ice surface, not to analyze, but just to admire. When a surface is totally covered in well-traced figures, it begins to look like a painting. It took me ten years of my life to learn how to make that painting.

Every once in a while, Barry, the fellow who usually drove the Zamboni, would come out and look with me. He is a good friend, and when he says "Keep it up, young fella," it means a lot. Especially at 1:00 AM.

4

LIFE AT THE WORLD LEVEL

I arrived in Ottawa in February for the 1987 Canadian championships knowing that I had to finish in the top three to qualify for that year's Worlds in Cincinnati. The practice sessions went well, increasing my confidence daily. I placed third in compulsory figures, bettered only by Orser and Neil Paterson—a real morale booster as we entered the original programs. Orser skated a phenomenal program, scoring six perfect 6.0s for artistic impression. But I managed to hold onto third spot overall, thanks to a triple Lutz combination that temporarily laid to rest my struggles with that particular jump.

The free skate was my best to date. Only Orser received

higher marks. I landed five triples, was marked in the 5.6 to 5.8 range and advanced to second place, standing beside Orser on the podium with the silver medal around my neck. As a bonus, Slipchuk came on strongly enough to win the bronze, ensuring that we'd be heading for the States together. The door to the world championships had swung open at last.

The Royal Glenora contingent—Slipper, Patsy Schmidt and I—along with our coaches, checked into Cincinnati's Terrace Hilton hotel. Each day, our rooms were filled with good-luck messages and gifts from the organizing committee and various sponsors, including a vitamin manufacturer. (As a result, we'd leave with a lifetime supply of wonder supplements.) Everyone was very buoyant, very upbeat. We couldn't wait to get to the practice rink, which had been set up in a convention center.

When people think of Cincinnati, they think of Orser and Boitano—round one in the unfolding "Battle of the Brians." The media attention that swirled around them left Slipper and me in the shadows. We were ecstatic just to be there, but nobody gave us a second glance, which explains why my activities that practice day didn't make the headlines.

The practice ice had been installed over a sort of styrofoam base, which made it feel springy and ideal for jumping. Boitano was obviously thinking about incorporating a quad into his program, but he and Orser were the prime contenders; they had far too much to lose. Orser was enjoying the extra-springy ice, too. All eyes were on him as he made an unusual approach to his next jump. The spectators were expecting something spectacular, and they weren't disappointed. Orser did the best quad I'd ever seen him do, though his landing was a bit shaky. The crowd went crazy.

Seeing this, I asked Mr. J. if I could try mine. Out I went and landed it perfectly. Nobody blinked an eye. I did a second, which seemed to arouse half-hearted interest in the spectators. I did a third, to sparse applause. I was totally baffled. I'd just done the impossible three times in a row. Admittedly, I'd done it on ice that seemed to have been cross-bred with a trampoline. The bounce from the styrofoam base gave me an unfair advantage, like a runner propelled by a tail wind. Still, I was upset—especially when I saw Orser's coach, Doug Leigh, and Mr. J. laughing their heads off at my obvious confusion.

Mr. J. called me over and patiently explained the situation. First, that year's glamor jump—the basis for comparison between Orser and Boitano—was the triple Axel. That's what the crowd had come to see, not a kid they'd never heard of turning four times in the air. In fact, most of the onlookers didn't know I'd been doing quads at all. That sounds stupid, but the quad happens so quickly that, if you do it cleanly, it looks like a triple toe-loop. The eye doesn't register four turns instead of three. Blink, and you miss an entire revolution. Even if they'd been watching me—with Orser on the ice—they'd think I was doing triples.

Those are facts of skating life, just like the fact that Slipper and I were the new kids on the ice. Well and good. We'd skate our hearts out and hope for the best. Realistically, though, I knew that a top-ten placement was beyond my reach. I hoped to finish in the top seventeen, the CFSA's cutoff point for its 1988 Olympic team. But the realities of judging at the world championship level were starting to sink in. On the first day of competition, I traced my compulsory figures as best I could, which wasn't great. I was twelfth on the first figure, nineteenth on the second and thirteenth on the third, finishing fourteenth overall.

The next day, Orser won the original program with a brilliant performance. After finishing second year after year, it looked as if this might be his chance to seize the crown. I could only stand and cheer him on, having placed nineteenth in the original program, due to a fall on my triple-double combination. That, combined with the figures, put me in seventeenth place as we entered the free-skating segment.

All eyes were on Orser and Boitano, with side bets on Alexandr Fadeev. I skated early in the day, finishing fourteenth in the free skate, with marks in the 5.0 to 5.3 range. This landed me a respectable fifteenth overall, enough to qualify for the Calgary Olympics. Slipper would rank twentieth, which teed him off, but we didn't have time to dwell on our showings. Like everyone else, our attention swung to the drama of the Big Three skaters.

Orser skated early in the final group, landing six triple jumps, two of them Axels. No one had ever landed two triple Axels in world competition before. He doubled out on a scheduled seventh triple, but his artistic marks were way up there. Still, it was possible for Boitano to beat him.

Boitano didn't play it safe. He tried a quad but fell on his landing, which was enough to ensure that Orser would take the gold. When Boitano went down, the Canadian team broke protocol with an involuntary shout. Fortunately, we were miles up in the stands, and I don't think it registered. You'll appreciate that it's not real great form to jump around when the other guy takes a tumble. Also, you don't want to see him fall, on general principle. You want him to stand up and take his best shot, beating him (if you can) with yours. In any case, Fadeev skated next, but he didn't have the leg strength to come on. He'd pulled a groin muscle three weeks before the competition. Very few people were aware of this, but those who were realized that the competition was strictly an Orser-Boitano showdown, despite a good performance from Chris Bowman.

And Orser took it, as he deserved, with Boitano second and Fadeev third. I cried when the results were posted. I can't get emotional about my own peformances, but I go overboard for skaters I respect. I remember standing down by the ice, babbling away to Mr. J. about wanting to have that moment myself some day.

I think we all considered ourselves fortunate to be Orser's teammates. The spotlight was on him; he took the pressure off our shoulders. We learned a lot from watching him—how he skated, how he conducted himself. He and I weren't close friends by any means. Back then, he was the senior statesman, and spent time with other skaters his own age. But I was so impressed by what he told the press on his victory night. "I had a mature attitude," he said. "I felt in control this week, from the very first figure. We had a well-defined strategy from day one. It feels wonderful to finally win. I've always wondered how winning the gold medal would feel, after seeing other competitors around me experience it." Well, now he knew. But I wondered, too, and resolved to be in his position someday.

Looking back on Cincinnati, I remember wonderful people, wonderful experiences. I was inspired by the Polish skater Grzegorz Filipowski, who finished fifth. I'd seen him at a Skate Canada meet when I was eleven or twelve years old, and now here we were, competing together. He did triple Axels all week long, closely monitored by me. Something must have registered. Three days after returning home, I started landing them cleanly in practice.

I celebrated with Tracy Wilson and Rob McCall, who'd won the ice dance bronze for a second straight year. Slipper and I wound up sitting on a sofa with Katarina Witt, who that year regained her women's title from Debbie Thomas. She watched the movie Cocoon on TV, while we watched her. Slipper and Scott Chalmers went on a beverage-hunting expedition across the river to Kentucky, returning with six-packs of something unspeakable, only to be nabbed by our team leaders John McKay and Marilyn Dunwoodie. (Actually, I was playing lookout man. I warned them to hide the booty, then embarked on a nonchalant conversation with John and Marilyn, oblivious to the fact that I still had my share of the liquid refreshments in my hand. Conspiracy is my life.)

Cincinnati also marked the debut of Lola the Doll. Doug Ladret had spent most of the season teasing Cynthia Coull, a pairs skater, by coming on to her in an outrageously flirtatious way. He chewed up the scenery, declaring eternal lust at every turn. Maybe the word "overblown" crossed Cynthia's mind. At any rate, she found a life-size inflatable doll and gave it to him as a consolation prize. Don't misunderstand me: Lola wasn't anatomically correct. In fact, she was a model lady—so much so that we took her with us on a Canadian Worlds Team tour of the Maritime provinces immediately afterward. Her wardrobe was something to behold; she figured prominently in our team pictures. Audiences loved her, especially when we sent her sailing into the crowd—kind of a Gumby-toss in reverse. But all good things come to an end, and so did Lola. I'm ashamed to say that I was responsible. Her arm broke during an extra-vigorous, extra-big throw triple Salchow in a show number we did together (I was never much good with a partner anyway), and Lola was never her old, blow-up self again.

One of the best years of my life was spent on Skid Row.

I'd met Sunil Vaidya in 1985 when I was dating Joelle Tustin. One of her friends was dating him, and the four of us went to a graduation dance. Sunil and I quickly became friends, and stayed friends after we'd broken up with the girls who'd introduced us. He was a contract estimator in real life; he'd do the costings on various construction projects. But he was also very good at sports, particularly soccer and baseball. I'd play on his teams whenever there was a last-minute opening, and we'd hang out at each other's apartments, renting a VCR and tapes from the 7-Eleven store and eating popcorn by the bushel.

Finally, in the fall of 1987, we awoke to the fact that, instead of paying $400 rent on two separate locations, we'd do far better to pool our resources and find a house. That's how Sunil, Kurt, Ian Ball and Dillip Koshy became joint tenants. We took the first letter from each of our given names and christened the place "Skid Row."

Mom arrived and gave us detailed instructions for whipping it into shape. Sunil and I shared the upper floor, while Ian and Dillip lived downstairs. The music was loud, the front door was always open. We were excellent hosts, which made for lively Saturday nights and busy Sunday mornings.

Sunil and I established a post-party routine. We'd stagger out of bed and set goals for the day. After breakfast, we analyzed the state of disrepair. One of us would take the kitchen, the other, the rest of our floor. Then we'd set a stopwatch, giving ourselves a time limit to impose order on chaos. (I think this was a throwback to when I was a kid and would put Mom's wristwatch on a fencepost. I'd race across the pasture and back, check the time elapsed, and then set off again, determined to better my record.) Our next stop was the Soaptime laundromat, where we'd pitch our clothes into the washers before heading outside to toss a football.

Looking back, I realize that Skid Row was my last chance to be lost in the shuffle, to feel anonymous and carefree. The next spring, when I landed my quad in Budapest, I battled millions of TV viewers by waving to the cameras and yelling "Hi, Skid Row!" One of the reporters was concerned; he wondered if I'd come from the wrong side of the tracks and consorted with winos and bums. Well, not exactly. I was just saying hello to twenty friends—all the people who'd helped us move in—who I knew were sprawled around our living room in Edmonton, probably with Def Leppard on the stereo for background noise, watching me skate my way into the Guinness Book of World Records.

The 1987-88 season was a make-or-break proposition. To qualify for the Olympic Games, I'd once again have to finish in the top three at the upcoming Canadians. I didn't see much of a problem there.

Mr. J. and Sandra Bezic, my choreographer, had helped me put together programs that they felt would enable me to reach my goal. The original program had evolved from a fun number I'd been doing in exhibitions to the tune "Tequila," a 1950s instrumental recorded by The Champs. The free skate, to Aaron Copeland's "Grand Canyon Suite," would take advantage of my legitimate western roots, and seemed a natural for Calgary.

The season started well, in September 1987, at the St. Ivel competition in Richmond, England, just outside London, where I won the silver medal.

In October, at the Skate Canada meet in Calgary, I tried a quad in front of judges for the first time, to get used to the idea of attempting it in a competition setting. I fell, but it didn't affect my placement. Orser beat Boitano, solidifying his Olympic prospects. Viktor Petrenko was third overall, and I came fourth, but I beat him in the free-skating segment, landing seven triples. Not bad, I thought, considering that he'd placed sixth in Cincinnati to my fifteenth. I felt tremendously encouraged. Here was concrete evidence that my training was paying off. To celebrate—and to provide a change of pace before the pre-Olympic push—we decided to accept a late invitation to join Nicky Slater's show tour of England and Ireland, along with Tracy Wilson and Rob McCall. This took place in December, but I was back in Caroline in plenty of time for Christmas, before a return to heavy training at the Royal Glenora in preparation for the Canadian championships in Victoria that February.

This time, my training involved more emphasis than ever before on compulsory figures. And, once again, it paid off. Only Orser and Neil Paterson scored higher.

Victoria was shaping up as a happy occasion. Tuffy and Doug won the pairs title the next day, and I rushed down to congratulate them. Watching Tuffy always put a smile on my face; she's never more beautiful than when she's on the ice. Their performance left me charged up for my own skate and seemed to bring me luck. Orser skated incredibly in the men's original, scoring seven perfect 6.0s for artistic impression. But I was in behind him, secure in second place.

The following day, as the free-skating finals were about to begin, the Olympic torch passed through Victoria on its way to Calgary. This should have charged me even more, but I think it had the opposite effect. I flubbed a triple Axel and decided not to try the quad, for fear of falling even further behind. I hadn't skated anywhere near my best. Nor, I think, had anybody else. Orser fell twice, but recovered to win his eighth consecutive senior title. Part of our problem was the ice, which was covered with a thin layer of water. This produced a very curious effect—I couldn't tell where the actual surface was—and it threw my timing off, so that my landings appeared awkward and unsure. Still, I managed not to fall out of contention and finished second overall.

As I stood on the podium with my silver medal, it hit me like a ton of bricks—my dream of Olympic competition had come true. The downside was that Slipper hadn't made it. Neil Paterson fought his way into third spot, skating at his best. Both he and Slipper went the limit that day. Actually, I felt that their individual performances were better than mine or even Brian's.

That was the moment that months of anxiety began to take their toll. Now that my place on the Olympic team was assured, I started to go to pieces. I went to the doping room, where we produce our urine samples, and quickly downed three or four bottles of beer. This did wonders for the sample, but not for my state of mind. Rob McCall was standing there, teasing Orser and me. "Pretty good free dance, guys," he said, meaning that, considering our lack of impressive jumps, we'd have been right at home in his dance event. There was nothing in the least malicious in his kidding; there never is. But at the time, it seemed that I was determined to take anything anybody said and turn it into a weapon against myself.

I was already late for the team reception at the hotel. Shelly Borden, from the CFSA, got me into a taxi and I headed down the road. After about a block I started crying. I couldn't understand what was happening to me. This was supposed to be a high point in my career. I'd made the Olympic team; I was going to skate for my country in my own backyard. I should have been running down the street in celebration. Instead, I was snuffling in the back seat of a cab and ticking off the negatives. My victory hadn't gone according to plan. I hadn't skated up to par. Slipper hadn't made the team. I was a sorry sight, no doubt about it. Then, when my cab pulled up in front of the hotel, the main event began.

By this time, the reception's organizers were in a mild frenzy, wondering what had become of me. I was well and truly late. Worse yet, David Dore, the CFSA's Director General, is a man who is truly fond of order and method. He had made certain arrangements, and everyone was going to stick to them, come hell or high water. I was informed that, as a medal winner, my presence was urgently and immediately required in the reception hall.

I had a suit of clothes upstairs, but I wasn't allowed to nip up in the elevator and change. Instead, I was ordered to stand around with the other skaters, wearing jeans, a bolo tie and a wrinkled shirt. Thanks to the doping-room beer, my breath was less than fresh. Everyone else had showered and changed and looked like a million dollars. I looked as if I'd come from—you guessed it—skid row. My eyes were swollen because I'd been crying non-stop during the taxi ride. People were looking at me sideways, wondering what I'd do next. I was utterly embarrassed and totally depressed, especially after I'd waited ten or fifteen minutes for the introductions to begin. In that time, I could have been upstairs and changed twice over. But no. I had to stand around, feeling like a fool, before being introduced. Then I had to circulate through a room full of skating officials and big-ticket corporate sponsors. If I'd hadn't been a rookie—low skater on the team totem pole—I'd have said, "Sorry, folks. I'm going to get suited up and blow my nose. See you in five. If the sky falls while I'm gone, too bad." Unfortunately, it didn't occur to me to do that at the time.

After the ceremonies, I went upstairs and sat in my room for a while. Then I went to Mom and Dad's room. They looked even more depressed than I did. I sat down, told them exactly what had happened and then cried for another solid hour. After that, I felt marginally better and decided that I could face my friends. Mom agreed. She told me to try to relax, to enjoy what was left of the evening. That was my next mistake. I found a party going on in Doug Ladret's room and started doing the rounds, trying to explain what had happened. After a while, somebody asked me to grab a couple of soft drinks from the balcony where they'd been keeping cool. I reached out, got the drinks, then tried to close the balcony door. But it was stuck, so I had to pull it harder. It slammed shut with a deafening crash. This brought Ladret on the run. When he saw who'd caused this new disturbance, he went through the roof.

In Doug's defence, he and Tuffy had been under tremendous pressure all that week as well. Not only had they gone through the struggle to make the team, they were now Canadian champions. I think they were a little overwhelmed by the sudden flood of new responsibilities. Doug was frazzled and touchy. He thought—following my behavior at the reception—that he had a lunatic on his hands. That didn't make what he had to say any easier to take. Roughly, he told me that he'd had it up to here with my complaining, my attitude and my general weirdness.

Plus, in his considered opinion, if I didn't appreciate being on the Olympic team, I shouldn't have made it.

That set me off again. I said he was unfair, that his own attitude left a lot to be desired, that if anybody was behaving weirdly, it wasn't me, and that if he wanted to talk like that, perhaps he should put his words into appropriate action. We stared at each other for a few seconds; then he walked away. His walking away was the best thing that happened that night.

I stood there, thinking, "What in heaven's name is going on?" What ought to have been a joyous occasion had fallen into ugly pieces. Later on, after we'd both had time to reconsider, Doug and I sat down and went over the whole week again, with emphasis on that night. Doug is certainly the person that we National Team skaters look up to as a leader. His words meant a lot to me. Happily, our friendship survived this episode, but I'd give anything if it hadn't happened, and I'm thankful that nothing quite that awful has ever happened again.

Four years ago, David Dore showed up at a national skating seminar and proceeded to rally the troops.

"If you don't win more medals," he said, "I won't have anything to go to sponsors with. If you don't win more medals, I won't have anything to get you the money you need. You won't go anywhere. We'll have to start cutting the number of skaters we send to competitions. So you've got to win more medals. Medals, medals, medals!" Each time he said the word, he chopped a forearm with his hand.

Dore made a profound impression that day. Long after that, every once in a while, when one of us won, we'd stand in the dressing room and chant "Medals, medals, medals!" at the top of our lungs.

Dore and I have clashed many times. He used to write me letters, expressing his fear that my quest to land the quad was getting out of hand. He was upset when he learned that

I was thinking about an agent. He was very upset when I finally got one, against his advice. At one competition, he kept looking at me strangely out of the corner of his eye. He kept saying to me and Matthew Hall, "This is it, boys. One mistake and it's all over. Curtains. Finished." This is the sort of style that endeared him to a generation of skaters.

Our team leader Carol Hopper said he had my best interests at heart, that he was trying to pull a good skate out of me. In fact, I was ready to hit him. Whatever he might have thought he was achieving, his technique wasn't working. There were many such instances—times when I felt he was meddling in my career to no good purpose. He was abrasive, authoritarian and aloof, like a very strict school principal. You respected him, because you knew he'd almost single-handedly built the CFSA into what it is today, but you feared him, too. Many skaters disliked him into the bargain.

I was lucky. After talking with Carol, I realized that Dore and I had to work together. I didn't have any choice, because I couldn't have this conflict. The change didn't happen overnight. Even at the 1989 Worlds in Paris, I can remember Mr. J. steering me around the CFSA contingent. But gradually, things began to change for the better. He was still the strict school principal, but the fear vanished, leaving the respect intact. Slowly, I realized that his concerns were genuine, that his comments and criticisms were coming from a caring place.

My theory is that Dore couldn't figure out how to handle me because he'd worked with Brian Orser for so long. Orser was around for ten years. For eight of those, he was the champion. That's a pretty good rut, but it's still a rut. When Orser retired, Dore didn't know what to make of me. I seemed flippant, as if I didn't care. I made him uneasy and preyed on his nerves. I didn't seem like a reliable product to sell. That's understandable. I wasn't Orser. Sometimes, I wasn't sure who I was. But then Dore came to understand and respect my own ambition. He made me focus and discover what it was I needed to achieve success. He played the devil's advocate. He made me question what I was doing, so that I didn't float aimlessly along.

Now I think we've come full circle. We can talk to each other honestly and candidly. I feel a bond with him; our relationship has evolved into a friendship. We're in a rut now, and the next champion will have to make his own way. But I can kid Dore without fear of misunderstanding. I call him "Super Dave," after the TV character. That's how I ask for him when I phone the CFSA headquarters. That's how he signs his handwritten letters to me.

I didn't exaggerate when I said that Dore almost single-handedly created the CFSA. It was his imagination and drive that took Canadian figure skating to a whole new level of public acceptance. The Skaters Development Committee was his brainchild. The national teams were under his control. He initiated the earliest TV deals. The funding came in because he convinced sponsors that skating was a good investment. His perseverance resulted in a level of corporate support that's the envy of other sports.

The CFSA can be tough, dogmatic and inflexible. It has to be. It's a very powerful body. It handles big money. It sells everything from TV time to rink-board advertising. It sells the entire competitive package, to sponsors and to the public. It sells us—the skaters on the national team. Without skaters who are on their feet, who are winning medals (medals, medals), who an audience wants to see, Dore has nothing to sell. The skaters know this. We aren't naive. The CFSA funds us through the various levels of competition, funnels us money from Sports Canada. We know that, without this money, we wouldn't go across the street, let alone to France and Germany and Japan. In this respect, Dore's done a great job.

Dore tries to instill in us a sense of responsibility, a sense of where the money comes from. Not only are we aware of the fact that we can't be naughty boys and girls, squandering our allowances, we know from a very early age that we have to be responsible for our own actions. We have to give the CFSA our time, go to skating parties, meet the sponsors and wear their sweaters. I have to make sure I don't have an individual sponsor that might clash with the national team's.

Just as the skaters have accepted these responsibilities, the CFSA members have become more supportive, more flexible. When I was having trouble in Halifax in 1989, they came to me and said, "Talk to us. Keep the lines of communication open. We're on your side. We want to be with you, not excluded." This atmosphere has been fostered by Dore.

At one of this year's team weekends, he ripped up the speech he was going to deliver. I'd called him, told him he was going to be in the book and read him some quotes, particularly "Medals, medals, medals!" In he walked, and he launched into a whole new address. He told the skaters that he wasn't down on them, that he didn't expect them to win at any cost. He simply laid out the facts, the CFSA's expectations and what he considered to be the skaters' obligations. And everyone responded to this. Dore has grown along with us. He listens. He tries. And no matter what happens, he'll always be Super Dave.

OTHER VOICES:

David Dore

In the early 1980s, when I was CFSA president, it seemed to me that many of our skaters were entering competitions and coming home somewhat pleased to have finished fifteenth. I attempted but failed to instill a more competitive attitude. In 1986, when I was hired as full-time Director General, I told skaters that they could in fact win, that they should not be satisfied with mediocre results.

In order to finance a viable world team, we needed to gain corporate sponsors. To attract sponsors, we needed medal-winning performances. I remember the speech that Kurt refers to. It might have sounded harsh, especially to the younger skaters, but I was convinced that there had to be a drastic change in direction.

In those days, Kurt was part of what I call the second generation of skaters. These younger people were in the shadows. Some of them felt that no one noticed them. This is because I was spending a great deal of time catering to the needs of our top skaters, and, because things were tight economically, driving hard bargains. I feared that people would harbor inaccurate perceptions of what I was trying to accomplish. I accepted a good deal of pressure, and in some cases transferred it to others. But even if Kurt and the others didn't realize it, I was always aware that they were there.

In 1984, Paul Martini and Barb Underhill won the world pairs title in Ottawa, bringing Canada its first gold medal since 1973. That same year, Brian Orser won the silver medal. These performances vindicated the world-team concept and provided a lift. We gained sponsors, but we had to keep the momentum going.

Over the next few years, skaters such as Orser, Liz Manley and our top pairs and dance teams continued to occupy my attention, but I saw Kurt and his peers as an integral part of the team's future. I can remember having discussions with various people about him. I became aware that he was a free spirit. He was much more independent, especially after he obtained an agent, than most of the other skaters, but he has always remained a strong team player. This has been a saving grace for us. I got used to letting him go his own way, which took some adjustment on my part. But he has never set himself above or outside the team.

Kurt has become an exceedingly popular role model for our up-and-coming skaters. His approach is determined but lighthearted, and that's all to the good; figure skating tends to take itself too seriously at times. He's terribly accessible—sometimes too much so—and has a magic way with young people. He can walk into a room full of Grade one kids and have them eating out of the palm of his hand.

He never bad-mouths anyone. He's never asked more from us than we can give. In fact, he's asked for very little. In return, he's given to the other skaters a feeling that they are valued, that things happen because of them.

This second generation of skaters has been just as, or more, successful than the first because of what they learned while awaiting their turn. Their attitude is very positive. I think that Kurt has cemented them together. Soon, a third generation will emerge and pick up where this group leaves off. Kurt's honesty and his inner strength have been important factors in this.

5

FINDING THE OLYMPIC SPIRIT

I had a theory about the Calgary Olympics. The skies would open, while perfection reigned supreme. I'd skate better than ever. Audiences would adore me. All this would happen just because it was the Olympics. But I was wrong. The ice felt the same. So did the jumps. So, for that matter, did the falls. The Games had always been associated in my mind with some exotic and far-off place. It was strange to realize that they were about to happen in my backyard, in a city that was so familiar to me. The mountains I could see were the same ones I saw from the front porch in Caroline.

I spent a month ironing the glitches out of my free-skating program. I also slipped in a weekend in Caroline, watched Wade's son J.J. play hockey, had dinner at cousin Jennifer's and shot pool with my friend Gareth Edwards. Mostly, though, I just kept plugging away at the Royal Glenora Club. Then, before I knew it, the Olympics were upon us.

The athletes received their official blazers at a reception attended by Brian and Mila Mulroney. Here I had my first encounter with Gaetan Boucher, the speed skater. He'd triumphed at the 1984 Games, and now, toward the end of his career, he was back to give it one more shot. When I saw him, I looked at Tuffy and Doug and the rest of us who were at our very first Olympics, standing beside a man who, in my mind, embodied the Olympic virtues. A whole city, a whole world, had come together for the Games, and that was wonderful—but so had two generations of athletes, who wouldn't otherwise have met.

There were sixty thousand people in McMahon Stadium to watch us march past in the opening procession. Brian Orser had been selected to lead the way, carrying the Canadian flag. The TV audience was estimated at two billion viewers worldwide, and we'd evolved a strategy that would put our faces on every set. The plan was to elbow our way to the outside of the reviewing track, putting us closer to the cameras. This would have worked nicely if we'd marched around clockwise, as anticipated. No sooner had we entered, however, than the parade marshals pointed us in the opposite direction, burying us on the inside of the pack.

We didn't really care, though. At least the suspense was over. We'd spent hours waiting for the procession to begin. We'd rallied at the arena, dressed for freezing winter weather, then sat inside, peeling off layers of clothing and falling asleep from the warmth. When we finally got the go-ahead, we had to get back into the outfits and walk a quarter-mile to the stadium. When we entered, costumed in red-and-white, the crowd went absolutely nuts.

Even while marching around the track, I felt curiously detached. I was waiting for the thunderclap, the special Olympic feeling to hit. Finally, Michael Farrington, the ice dancer who skated with Melanie Cole, poked my ribs and said, "Hey, someone's yelling your name." I don't know how he heard; you couldn't hear yourself think amid the noise. I looked up to see my brother and sister in the stands. Their faces were the catalyst, the icing on the cake that made a perfect day.

That night, the team went to Canada House, which was an off-site refuge. It was an actual house, away from the Olympic Village. That's where you went to relax, to meet your parents or get a good night's sleep, to escape for a minute from the pressure-cooker. We had a pizza party and watched a tape of the opening ceremonies. The cameras had failed to pick me up, but there were several shots of Tuffy, who had a habit of cocking her head to one side when she smiled at people. She'd been smiling non-stop all through the procession, and we teased her about doing "the Tuffy Tilt" on two billion television sets.

No events were scheduled for the next day, so Neil Paterson and I watched the Czechoslovakian hockey team in practice, played video games and mastered the electronic message-boards—computer terminals set up on every other floor of the dormitories that enabled us to punch up people's names and send them good-luck greetings, exchange vital information or simply fool around. By entering your own name, you could receive all the messages that had been left for you. We were in constant touch with everyone from Andy Moog, the Edmonton Oilers goaltender, to the girls who worked in the laundry.

Compulsory figures were traced at the Father David Bauer Arena early the following day. I placed eleventh—not bad, but a minor disappointment. I'd hoped to be in the top ten. The Olympic rules required us to undergo a doping test after both the figures and the original program, instead of at the end, the way it's done at other competitions. The unfamiliar procedure made for a long and tiring day that started to fray my nerves.

As a result, I felt edgy and unsure the day of the original program. I started losing concentration and botching jumps at my practice. Mr. J. was working on the technical tune-up, calm and secure as usual. He didn't seem upset, but I was rattled, afraid that I was going to disgrace myself in front of an Olympic audience. I grabbed his arm and shouted, "I'm scared. Really scared. You've got to help me." He stared at me with a very odd look, and then he began to laugh, which wasn't the kind of help I had in mind. "This isn't funny!" I said. "Yes, it is," he replied. "Why do we work so hard? So you can skate in front of people. Why do you jump, over and over again? So you can go to competitions like this one. You were second at the Canadians. You earned the right to compete here today. Now you're telling me that you want to worry about it? Look—the work is done, it's over. You're at the Olympic Games. I don't care how you skate as long as you have fun and enjoy it."

I looked at him blankly; I didn't grasp what he was saying. It wasn't his usual pre-competition lecture, that's for sure. But, as usual, it was exactly the right thing to say. It made sense. Maybe the Games were a once-in-a-lifetime thing. Who was to say I'd qualify for another try? So I took his advice, calmed down and promised myself that I'd relax and simply do my best.

Easier said than done. By the time it was my turn to skate that evening, I was nervous as a cat all over again—but this time in a positive way. I was the final skater in my group. Everyone before me had skated cleanly, and here I was, the home-town boy, warming up by pretending I was someplace else, over-rotating double Axels and bumping into the boards. To my surprise, when I actually began the program, things went well. "Tequila" was a definite crowd-pleaser.

I began by miming its opening guitar chords. Afterward, I felt that I'd been overcautious. I wasn't as dynamic as I might have been. Still, I received seventh-best marks, moving to ninth place overall. Orser and Boitano, as expected, were one-two at the top of the standings.

That night, I stayed late at the village, burning off nervous energy. Chris Bowman was the toast of the town that night! He was ready to celebrate. The next day was free time, and I spent part of it hanging around with the Canadian bobsled team. Neil Paterson and I watched a hockey game. This was the great part of being in the Olympic village—the mix of different athletes. At a skating competition, all you can think about is skating. There's no escape; that's all there is. In Calgary, I could walk down the hall and bump into somebody who was totally consumed by his own event, about which I knew zip. All I could do was cheer him on, and that in itself was a wonderful relief. It pulled me away from thinking about what I had to do.

The bobsledders, led by Chris Lori, were on our floor. In my mind, I'd always put them in the same category as skaters; they had to be agile and have good balance. I didn't think of them as particularly strong. Wrong. These guys are in amazing shape. They've got huge chunks of muscle, and I know how they get them. It comes from sharpening the runner that goes underneath a sled. They would detach it and bring it up to their rooms. Then, while they watched TV, they'd take out any scratches, using progressively finer grades of sandpaper. I tried this for about two and a half minutes, until my whole arm started burning. You have to push hard, really leaning into it. They'd sand away for forty-five minutes straight. Just watching them tended to put your own event in perspective. So did the presence of the Jamaican bobsled team, wearing parkas, and Eddie the Eagle, the kamikaze English ski jumper who got more than his share of press coverage.

The day of the free-skating final, the temperature rose to record heights. Inside the arena, a crowd of almost twenty thousand people sat in sweltering conditions. After my warm-up (the word sounds peculiar, given the heat), I was burning. I slipped away under the stands, stripped my outfit—a one-piece zippered jumpsuit—to my knees and stood there in my jockstrap, slapping wet towels all over my body, aided by Mr. J. and Rosemary Marks, who was now our assistant team leader. Situations like these help make skaters one big, happy family. After the cold compress routine, I felt great, ready to step back onto the ice and go for Olympic glory.

Just before my entrance, Paul Martini, who'd won the world pairs title in 1984 with Barb Underhill, grabbed my arm. He was doing color commentary for a TV network. (It's a pity he missed my under-the-boards striptease!) "Don't go straight to your starting spot," he said. "Skate around a little bit first. The crowd is going to clap forever when you go out. Waste some time. You don't want to stand there too long before your music starts."

I took his advice, and it was good thing I did. When the audience caught sight of me, they gave me a tremendous ovation. I skated around in circles, glad that Martini had tipped me off. If I'd had to stand there motionless, I'd have lost all concentration.

My free-skating program, to "Grand Canyon Suite," went quite well. Its western theme further enthused the crowd. I was the only skater to attempt a quad, but I fell. Still, I completed seven triple jumps and placed sixth, to finish eighth overall—a top-ten showing, which was all I really wanted.

Unfortunately, Orser lost this installment of the "Battle of the Brians," finishing second to Boitano, while Petrenko won bronze. Orser's problems began with Boitano's skate, which appeared to be unbeatable. Ten minutes later, it was Orser's turn. He rose to the challenge, but, toward the end of his program, he turned a scheduled triple jump into a double. This might have been the deciding factor. Boitano received top marks from five of the nine judges; Orser was placed higher by the other four. The end result was heart-breakingly close. One-tenth of a point had decided the Olympic championship.

Orser had style, even in defeat. At the news conference, he said that he'd given it his best shot, that he felt he didn't have to apologize for anything. He was right! I wish he had decided to do the second triple Axel, but after almost every skate there's something you wish you could do over again. I don't mean to slight Orser in any way. He won the title of the best free skater in the world many times over. I'm still striving to approach the sheer genius of his programs.

Looking back on Calgary, I realize that I was as happy about just being there as I was about my skating or my placement. What I hardly thought about, because the Olympics were so exciting, was that I'd placed seven spots higher than at the Cincinnati Worlds. But I'd tried a quad and failed to land it. I still had work to do.

For the moment, though, my job was done, and I could forget about myself and cheer others on. I watched Wilson and McCall capture the ice dance bronze. Then Rod Garossino and I did our part to help Liz Manley win the women's silver medal by starting a wave among the audience. All of us were so happy that she'd rebounded from some very depressing times. She deserved her success that day. I'd always been impressed by the fact that she went out of her way to make me feel comfortable, back when she was Canadian champion and I was a complete nobody. Just before the Cincinnati competition began, she showed me and Slipper her tattoo, a little CFSA skate blade on her hip. We felt as if we'd undergone an initiation, become part of the team, all because of that cute and personal gesture. I liked her a lot, even though our paths didn't cross very often. She was so alive, so full of fun—a little fire-pot that

can sometimes bubble right over. She went on to a successful professional career, and nobody deserves the payback
as much as she does.

The last few days in Calgary were a time for relaxation,
an opportunity to socialize with everyone I'd met. The
entire city was in a party mood. If you were seen wearing
your team jacket, the red carpet went out in earnest. One
night, British skater Cheryl Peake and I were late for our
appointment at a club downtown. Cheryl promptly dialed
the nearest police station. I was horrified, but she explained
that policemen were our friends and would be honored to
provide an escort. "Maybe your London bobby is keen to
chauffeur you around," I said, "but I'm afraid it doesn't
work that way in Canada." I was wrong. A cruiser showed
up in no time flat. I was busy apologizing and trying to
send the policeman away to catch crooks, but he ordered
us to hop in, drove us to the club and pulled up in a blaze
of lights and sirens. It so happened that his son worked at
the club, where we were handed free drinks and danced
the night away.

Looking back on Calgary, I spent far more hours dancing than doing triple loops. I also jumped off the ten-meter
board at the Village pool, so as not to be upstaged by Todd
Gillman, the ski jumper, who risked his neck to impress the
female skaters. I remember the hockey players who qui-
eted down an entire floor of our residence so that Orser
could sleep the night before his free skate. I remember
giving k.d. lang an onstage hug during her concert and
attracting TV coverage with my unique dance style, to the
dismay of my partner, Karyn Garossino. And I remember
landing one of my patented "waxels" at the post-competition gala in the arena, then racing madly to the stadium for
the closing ceremonies, where the Olympic flame was
extinguished and the youth of the world was invited to
reunite in Albertville, four years down the line. A security
guard had to prevent me and Denise Benning, a pairs

skater, from making a dash across the field. As it was, we had to settle for seats on the far sideline.

I was looking at the flame when Donald Jackson appeared in front of us. I don't know how he found me in the crowd, or why he said to me what he did. He must have known what was on my mind. He spoke for less than thirty seconds, but I can hear him now. You'll remember that he was the first to land a triple Lutz in competition. That night, however, he talked about my quest for the quad. "Don't worry about it," he said. "Just do it next time. I can't tell you what it's going to do for you. You have to do it, to find out for yourself. Trust me. It's unbelievable. After I did my Lutz, so many things happened for me. All I can tell you is, just do it." Then he moved away, and the celebrations rolled on, leaving me even more determined in my mind about what would happen next.

6

HISTORY IN EIGHT-TENTHS OF A SECOND

Here is what happens when I do the quadruple toe-loop, also known as the quad. I turn four times in the air at a speed of three-hundred revolutions per minute—almost ten times faster than a long-playing record. From takeoff to landing, I travel at least twelve feet across the ice. I'm airborne eight-tenths of a second. If you've seen pictures of me in midair, you'll notice that I look somewhat less intelligent than usual. In fact, I look very strange. That's because my face is distorted by the speed. My center of gravity shifts. I push off from one foot and land on another. Nobody has calculated with accuracy the force of that impact. Nobody has figured out exactly how much thrust I need to get up. There's so much power involved—not raw, unfocused power, but pointed, purposeful force. The intensity is amazing. You can feel every muscle waiting and waiting. Then, if you put them into action at the right moment, you explode. It's a great feeling. You know you've hit it the moment you leave the ice, like a baseball player who swings, connects and just stands there for a second, knowing the ball is long gone for a home run.

I've been asked what goes through my mind when I'm up there. Not too much. Eight-tenths of a second goes by fairly quickly; you don't have time to spare. It's sort of like a midway ride; the world is spinning around me. I can feel, rather than see, the stands. I'm working on instinct. I try to fix a horizontal plane—the top of the boards, or people's faces. They're all a blur, of course.

If you under-rotate the quad, the fall can be particularly unpleasant. I don't fall as often practicing the quad as I do on other jumps, but when I do, the force usually makes up for the rarity.

I'd been landing quads in practice for a couple of years. I'd landed them in Cincinnati and tried them here and there, whenever I felt the chance existed. Other people were landing them, too. But there are two important distinctions that put my name into skating history. I was the first to land a quad perfectly and cleanly—landing on one foot, not two—at a recognized, sanctioned skating event. Not fooling around in practice, not on springy ice, not on a pond in the middle of nowhere without a battery of judges around. That is why my name is in the Guinness Book of World Records. I was the first to do it. I won't be the last.

Let's be clear about this. Skating folklore is rich with jumps that never happened, real fish stories. According to legend, there have been quad Salchows and fantastic combination leaps. Perhaps people were landing quads in some manner during the 1940s, because that's when the rumors began to circulate. Josef Sebovcik, a Czechoslovakian, was doing quads quite early on. He's a skinny guy with no apparent muscles, and he can jump like the wind. Once he was so close on his landing it was difficult to tell. All he was missing was a perfect landing in competition. Still, he's one of the most exciting jumpers I've ever seen. Boitano did a perfect quad in practice at St. Gervais. I've seen Orser do them. But I was the first to hit one when it counted.

Why did none of these people beat me to it? As I've explained, they hesitated to try the quad because they were very cool and calculating competitors. They placed a premium on doing clean programs. They didn't want to be seen failing in that very evident way. I didn't have that frame of mind. If I missed, it was no big deal; I had relatively little to lose. I wasn't as consistent as they were, and probably never would be. Nonetheless, with so many people trying it in practice, wanting to prove that it could be done, somebody was bound to do the quad in competition before too long. It became a race, like waiting for the first transatlantic flight.

Shortly after the Olympics, Mr. J. and I had a talk about it and decided that it was time for me to put up or shut up. We wrote a quad into my free-skating program—up near the front, about twenty seconds in—and decided that I'd attempt it at the 1988 world championships in Budapest. My Dad was glad to hear it. He'd had about enough of the speculation. When I was about to leave, he made it plain that if I didn't do it, we'd never talk about it again, because he was getting fed up hearing about it—and he wasn't the only one!

I started feeling better about the prospect every day. Once we'd slotted it in the free skate, I practiced it more and more. One afternoon at the Royal Glenora, the week before I left for Hungary, I nailed seven of them, one after the other. I was as ready as I was ever going to be.

On arrival in Budapest, I learned that Vladamir Kotin, the Soviet skater who'd placed fourth in Cincinnati and sixth at the Olympics, had withdrawn. This put me in a position to move up a notch from my eighth-place Olympic finish. The quad was well and good, but the main thing was to advance my world ranking.

Everyone was positive and upbeat, which is natural, given the momentum that we'd built up at the Olympics barely a month before. But the compulsory figures brought me down to earth with a jolt. I placed twelfth, and Orser struggled too, finishing fifth. Alexandr Fadeev won the figures but aggravated his pulled groin muscle and bowed out of competition. As a result, I was more or less assured of a top-ten berth, even before I laced my skates. If I could land the quad, my chances of a higher placement would improve dramatically. My luck held into the original programs, where Boitano edged out Orser for the top rung and I finished seventh, moving to ninth place overall, cheered by the fact that I was knocking off quad after quad during practice sessions.

Away from the rink, we'd seize every opportunity to explore the city. This was our first glimpse of a Communist country. Tuffy and I went jogging past old gray buildings, still marked by damage sustained during the Second World War. All the cars were boxy and tinny-looking, painted in drab monotones. The weather was overcast, adding to a sense of gloom. Still, we managed to seize a shopping opportunity or two. Orser and I went out one day to scout the stores. He bought a pair of painted ceramic vases. As it happens, he jumped the gun a bit, because the exact same vases turned up as our gifts at the Parade of Champions.

The day of the free-skating final, Neil Paterson and I were hyper. (Neil was Canada's third men's singles entry.) We felt like six-year-olds with a bag of Hallowe'en candy. We kicked a soccer ball up and down the hotel corridor before walking to the stadium, where we watched Katarina Witt, Caryn Kadavy and Jill Trenary—three gorgeous girls who interrupted their practice to wish me luck.

I'd have been content to watch them skate for the rest of the afternoon, but Mr. J. arrived and dragged me over to the main rink for my warm-up. We'd arranged that I'd start and finish it with plenty of time to spare. Those were the days when I'd get so excited during the warm-up that I'd experience a letdown between it and the competition. As it happened, I was glad that we called a halt. I walked over to the "kiss-and-cry" area, where the skaters await their marks. Mr. J. came along, and we sat down to talk. Suddenly, I held up my hand, only to discover that it was shaking like a leaf. Not unnaturally, Mr. J. was alarmed and asked me if I was okay. I waited for a second while my heart rate came back down. Then I looked at him and said, "Yeah. I'm ready."

"Well, then," he said. "Let's do it."

I glided back onto the ice and went through my pre-skate ritual. First, I touched base again with Mr. J. He ran through about a dozen of his standard comments: "One thing at a time. Get as many points as you can. Nail it. Be strong." Then I did a knee bend and stamped my blades before moving to center ice. Aaron Copeland's *Grand Canyon Suite* came out of the speakers, and my free skate was underway.

I had less than half a minute before the quad attempt. Every crossover, every turn, was building to that moment. As I made my approach, I had the weirdest thought: I felt curious about what was going to happen. I thought, "This is so exciting. Everyone is waiting to see if I can do it. I wonder if I can." I wasn't the least bit nervous. I had a wait-and-see, almost fatalistic attitude.

I went up really well. The spark that ignites to propel me high and fast enough kicked in. I was up and down—on one foot—in an instant. I knew I'd made the four revolutions and started congratulating myself. As a result, I almost blew the landing. I came down from the jump with tremendous torque and started to over-rotate. I did a three-turn, to regain my balance. I thought, "Oh, no. They aren't going to count it. Yes, I got the revolutions. Yes, I got the one foot down. Then I lost control. All that work and effort, to come so close." That made me very angry, but I couldn't stop. I put that angry energy into my next jump, a triple Axel. Then I started to hear the screams. I looked over to our team. Everyone was going wild, standing up and cheering. I thought, "Well, maybe I made it." I tore into the rest of the program, including six more triples. It's still one of my favorite programs ever. It was powerful and clean, a joy to remember, and a joy to perform that day.

Josef Dedic, a vice-president of the International Skating Union, verified that the quad would count. I was in the record books, along with Donald Jackson, Vern Taylor (the first skater to land a triple Axel in competition, in 1978) and Petra Burka (the first woman to complete a triple Salchow at the Worlds, in 1965).

The judges gave me 5.7s and 5.8s for technical merit and 5.5s to 5.8s for artistic impression. This raised me to third spot in the free skate, behind Orser and Boitano, and meant that I would finish sixth overall.

I've been asked: All right. You just cracked the Guinness Book of World Records. Didn't that mean your marks should have been through the roof? What's all this about 5.7s and 5.8s for technical merit? Let me answer this way. I remember once, at the NHK competition, watching Alexandr Fadeev at the top of his form. He didn't look as if he was moving very fast, but he went by you like a shot. His footwork was extraordinary in every detail. He had good carriage and poise. Everything was clean and crisp. There was absolutely no sense of strain or apparent effort. He floated; he was truly masterful.

Those are the things I didn't have in 1988. Fine. I did a quad, but Orser and Boitano were better skaters. If you looked at Boitano's spins and mine, there was no comparison in their quality. And our choreography was miles apart. I was a kid out there doing a cowboy number; I wasn't a polished world champion. I wasn't prepared for what was coming next. Believe me, when I saw the 5.7s and 5.8s come up, my mouth fell open and I punched Mr. J. in the shoulder. I was ecstatic. Those marks were completely fair, and my third-place finish in the free skate was the best I could have hoped for. Before they abolished figures, there were medals awarded to the top three free-skate placings; that tiny bronze medal is something I'm very proud of. It inspired me in Paris the following year; it was another link in the chain. So was the quad, when you come right down to it. It helped make my reputation, but it wasn't the end of the line.

Actually, the guy who should have made the record books that day, for the most hilarious interview question, was a broadcaster named Ted Green. What he said, to the best of my recollection, was, "A lot of people say they're going into the bush to wrestle a bear, but nobody really does it. You did it. How do you feel?" I burst out laughing. I felt as if the bear had popped out of the shrubbery, carrying a microphone.

Nothing happens in isolation. For one thing, Orser and Boitano were yet to skate. Orser did beautifully, beating Boitano in the free skate, but he finished behind him overall. Boitano tried a quad but two-footed the landing. Still, he took the gold, based on his showings in figures and his original program. Actually—and this gets somewhat technical—I had hopes, delusions really, of beating Boitano in the free skate. If Orser and one other skater had beaten him, Orser would have won, on cumulative points. Liz Manley won the women's silver, while Wilson and McCall repeated as bronze medal winners in the ice dance.

The significant thing was that all of these medallists then retired from competition, leaving the field open for me and the next generation. It was a clean slate, a whole new ball game. It enabled me to start formulating a new game plan. With the two guys who beat me out of the picture, I

85

had a far better chance at the next year's Worlds in Paris. I'd already started planning for the future.

In a way, I was sorry I hadn't landed the quad in Calgary, at the Olympics. That would have been an incredible experience—to do it in Canada, in front of a home-town crowd. But, if I'd done that, I might have been lost in the Olympic shuffle. From a purely self-serving standpoint, it was better to do it when the spotlight was entirely on skating, as opposed to every sport under the sun. That way, a little bit more of the spotlight landed and remained on me.

The rewards weren't long in coming. One of the most important was waiting for me at my hotel. It was a telegram, reading: "Wish I could have been there. Congratulations on making skating history. Now that the quad is under your belt, keep the rest of the world trying to catch up."

It was signed Donald Jackson.

Here I am at fifteen months on my first horse, Sham. They start them early on the Browning ranch.

Never shy of the camera! Except whoever did my makeup for this big photo shoot didn't notice I was drooling!

Above: On my first holiday in Mexico with Mom and Dad. By the look on my face, I think I missed Sham!

Below: I had all the essentials of hockey—skates, stick, puck, gloves, a helmet and *warmth*!

Above: No draft for this team! Playing Tiny Mite in Caroline—I'm fourth from the right, the only kid with a comb!

Below: My first and only skating partner, Michelle Pollitt, and I as pre-juvenile dance champions of Alberta, 1978.

Right: Picture day for the Rocky Carnival, where I skated for five years.

Below: Competing at the novice level at divisionals en route to the 1982 Canadians. Norm Proft, in blue, and Douglas Hemmerling are still good friends.

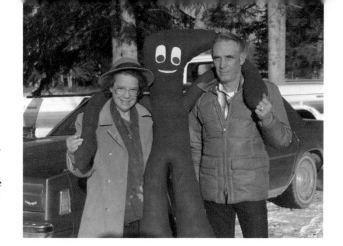

Mom and Dad and a hitchhiker we picked up on the way to Moose Jaw for the 1985 divisionals.

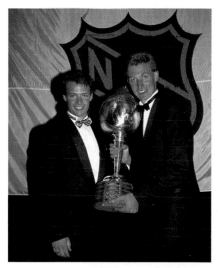

Left: Wayne saw my Mom and I watching his press conference and invited us up to take a few pictures. Another classy Wayne move, this time off the ice.
(Photo courtesy of Bruce Bennet.)

Below: Meet my coach and one of my best friends for the past eleven years, Michael Jiranek.
(Photo courtesy of Gerry Thomas.)

Left: See, David Dore
isn't as scary as some of
you may think. Meet the
Alan Eagleson of figure
skating.
(Photo courtesy of
Athletic Information
Bureau.)

There was a sale on used jackets and hats in Calgary just before the
opening ceremonies. Who knew? They're tiny, but they're there. Have
fun finding them! Tracy Wilson, Karyn Garossino, Kellie Kasey, Nancy
Gee, Karen Percy, Denise Benning, Charlene Wong, Michelle McKendry,
Kevin Albrecht, Lucy LeRoche, Horst Bulau, Rob Boyd, Me (waving at
Wade), Michael Farrington, Rod Garossino, Lloyd Eisler, Neil
Patterson, Doug Ladret. Front row: "Bobbers" (bobsledders).
(Photo courtesy of Wade Browning.)

The fun begins. Playing the invisible guitar at the opening of my "Tequila" program in the "Corral" at the Olympics.

Above: It was time to celebrate after landing the quad in Budapest. Getting a hug from teammates Melanie Cole and Liz Manley. Tuffy is hiding behind Melanie.

Below: Wearing our Maritime sweaters in Halifax. When I made the world team, I also made many friends for life.

7

A CANADIAN
IN PARIS

Katarina Witt had won a fourth world title to match her
two Olympic golds. Along with Orser and Boitano, she
announced her retirement from competitive skating.

The International Skating Union's fifteen-city champions tour of Europe became her farewell showcase, and I
was invited along. These tours were an annual event
immediately following the world competition. They were
basically fund-raisers to keep the skating union going. You
were expected to take part: if you won Worlds, you went
on the ISU tour. Some itineraries were truly hair-raising,
involving thirty shows in seventeen countries in forty-five
days. This one was, by comparison, leisurely.

Every night, the arena announcer would introduce me as the man who'd landed the quad. I must have heard this in a dozen different languages. Somehow, the word "quad" always sounded more or less the same.

The tour began in Czechoslovakia. Petr Barna, my roommate, was from Prague and acted as emergency interpreter. We arrived at Karvina, on the northern border with Poland, to find that we'd been billeted in a State-run rehabilitation center, which made for a change of pace. After checking in, I had an iodine bath in a mammoth metal tub, then fell asleep in a highly tranquil state.

I was woken from my deep, floating sleep by a large, sturdy Czech woman who helped me out of the huge tub. The fact that I had no clothes on whatsoever bothered me a lot more than it did her. After I wrapped myself in a towel I was able to enjoy a therapeutic, but rough, massage. So this was tour life?

The first show of a tour is always difficult; there are opening-night nerves and the inevitable technical glitches. A few small things are almost guaranteed to go wrong. My music was played at breakneck speed, and I struggled to keep up with it.

That night happened to be Chris Bowman's twenty-first birthday. Back at the rehab center, we rolled out a cake, while a band played on the top floor. Witt was there with bells on. She loved to dance—it's about the only thing we had in common—and so we spent most of the evening together.

Actually, I think I was a stand-in that night for Patrick Swayze, the star of the movie *Dirty Dancing*. Katarina thought he was terrific. She watched a videotape of the film over and over again and played the soundtrack tape at every opportunity. This was a bit too much of a good thing—especially when she decided that the shows should be renamed "the Dirty Dancing Tour." Put that in a postcard home, and see how friends and family rejoice in your success!

Witt had always been under the watchful eye of her

coach, a woman named Jutta Mueller, who had directed her every move, both on and off the ice. Now, however, with Witt's competitive days a thing of the past, Mueller relaxed the reins. It was this atmosphere that allowed me to get to know her better.

I was totally unlike her usual admirers. At five-foot-seven, I didn't exactly tower above her. I was younger than she was; I certainly wasn't rich and famous. I had a preconceived idea of what I thought she should be like. It took me a while to open up to the fact that I was wrong.

Strangely, Jutta Mueller didn't mind my being on the scene. Even more strangely—considering that she'd reduced countless other skaters to a state of mortal fear—she and I became friends as well. I discovered that she had a sense of humor. The following year, in Paris, when I remarked that her new skaters seemed very talented, she said, "But Kurt, they are much too young for you!"

So that's how Katarina and I hit it off. Everyone else was quick to assume that I was in her clutches. Orser told me to beware. "Don't start liking her," he said. "Every guy she meets falls in love with her." He needn't have worried. I was far more curious than amorous, because there was a lot to be curious about.

Witt could be hard as nails, no question about it. She'd elevated her defense mechanisms to an art form. There were always so many people pushing at her, and because of this she wouldn't try to connect with her fans. She signed autographs with a fixed smile, never looking people in the eye. She was willful and capricious. Once, when we were out to dinner, she sent back her meal because she'd noticed a more attractive-looking entrée on someone else's table. She was impulsive and did things on a whim, but because of her charisma she got away with it—no problem. The team's image rested on her shoulders. She'd been used, and she dealt with it in her own way. She knew how to sell herself, how to play cat-and-mouse with the press, how to put together fashion looks in ten seconds flat.

She was fascinating to be around, because she made things happen. Once we went to a bar and were ushered into a special section, the center of attention. You felt honored to be with someone who wielded that kind of power. It was my first contact with someone whose personality went beyond mere charisma, all the way to star-quality.

Her defense mechanisms can get her in and out of trouble. One night, Mueller had arranged a celebrity date for her. This guy was some kind of minor royalty. He drove an Alfa Romeo and appeared to be rolling in money. At the end of the night, I think he expected a little more than he got. Katarina felt no remorse in brushing him off. When you are as famous and as beautiful as Katarina, it must be difficult to meet people and trust their intentions.

On another occasion, during a show stop in Italy, she embarrassed the Italian skier Alberto Tomba, who'd won two gold medals at the Calgary Olympics. At that time, the media presented him as hot on Katarina's trail. Now, a TV team lured her toward him in the arena. The interviewer reintroduced them and asked her to give him a kiss for the camera. Katarina looked at him coldly and said, "What sport are you in?" In fact, she remembered exactly who he was, but she was determined not to be manipulated by the media.

The next day, we were aboard a bus, heading for Berlin. We stopped for coffee, and several people came back with the tabloid newspapers. A front-page photo showed Katarina helping me change my shirt during the previous day's show. The photo had been very creatively cropped. You couldn't tell where we were, and the end effect was fairly racy. The story went on to claim that Tomba and I had been in a fistfight over Katarina's favors. Another photo showed Katarina and me feeding each other ice cream. The caption said we'd escaped through the back door of the restaurant, en route to a secret rendezvous.

This sort of thing proved too much for Jutta Mueller. She began to stake out Katarina's room, and her surveillance intensified. Petr Barna was delighted by these developments. He wandered around saying, "Katarina whistles, Kurt jumps," in a mournful voice. Orser was busy counting the hours and minutes till the wedding day. Eventually, of course, the press found a new fun couple to speculate about, the tour continued, and Katarina and I remained good friends.

Touring is a world apart from competition, a world unto itself. It's a rewarding but disorienting experience. Skaters are thrown suddenly together. Then, just as suddenly, it's closing night, and the next time around, all the names and faces may have changed.

While the tour is under way, you skim the surface of wherever you happen to be. You might see only a four-block radius around your hotel. Rest is the priority. You're more concerned about falling asleep than asking the concierge what there is to see, catching a bus and seeing it. You fall asleep because you have a show to do that night in front of six thousand people, and you don't want to fall down. Quite often, you sleep the day away. When you do get out, it's usually after the show. It's late at night and you're wide awake. You can't go to museums and art galleries. The only places that are open are the nightclubs. So you go dancing, meet some local people at the club, and that's it—another world capital off the list. For example, that's all I remember about Karvina. After we'd blown out the candles on Chris Bowman's cake, we went downtown, playing Jets and Sharks from *West Side Story*, singing a parody of "Maria." I wound up in a tiny, very noisy club, dancing in a circle with Katarina Witt and a sixty-five-year-old Czechoslovakian lady.

I try to take mental snapshots; you hold onto what memories you can. Some cities went by in a blur, and I can't be certain I was in them. Others can be summed up in a sentence, a paragraph. In Venice, I went shopping with Lyndon Johnston (a wonderful skater who deserves a less controversial name). Guys don't usually enjoy superior shopping trips, but this one was fantastic. We took a gondola, whose owner handled it like a New York taxicab. We met a gypsy woman, who gave us the evil eye. We were wearing neon shorts; everyone else was in impeccably tailored jackets. We sat on the edge of the canal, waving to tourists in glass-topped boats. Then we blundered into a tailor's shop, bought impeccably tailored jackets of our own and received a standing ovation from the rest of the tour members when they caught sight of our new and improved wardrobe.

In Brussels, I found myself in a real red-light district. The working girls displayed themselves in windows, surrounded by harsh neon lights. They looked supremely bored; many kept busy by knitting. When they saw you coming, they'd whip off their tops. If you displayed no immediate sign of wanting to try their wares, they'd put the tops back on again—all of which was fascinating for a small-town Canadian boy.

I remember the harbor in Copenhagen, where I sat on the docks with Petr Barna and talked about our childhoods. Our hotel was down by the waterfront. I could open up the window and see ships from all over the world, sailors who looked exactly like Popeye. In Helsinki, I saw the movie *Fatal Attraction*. And that was about it for Finland.

This London story actually happened a year later, but I want to tell you about it now. It shows the hazard of taking things for granted on foreign shores. I had three hours between practices, so I thought I'd go jogging. No problem there. How could I possibly go wrong if I ran along the Thames? I crossed over one bridge and headed down the opposite bank. I knew I could get back where I started from. There were plenty of bridges in London. I'd seen pictures of them.

Pretty soon, I began to feel on top of the world. I was alone in London, having a wonderful time. I started to veer away from the riverbank. After a while, I realized that I wasn't in central London any more. I didn't know where I was, but it didn't look promising. That's when I found a bridge and crossed over. Good! But the route back was under construction. I had to keep leaving the path by the river. I'd lost track of the Thames, but not of the time. I was definitely late. I found the river again by running through the yard of an apartment building.

Now at least I was in a residential neighborhood. The houses had backyards that ran down to the river's edge, divided by fences and hedges. I was leap-frogging over shrubs and low brick walls. Then I came up against a towering hedge. It was seven or eight feet high; no way I was going over it. I had to get back to the road, but I was stuck in someone's garden. There was a gate at the side of the house, but it was padlocked. Trapped! Then I noticed that I could see right through the house. The back door led to a hallway that led to the front door that led to the street. Both doors were wide open. The owners may or may not have been home, working in the kitchen. If anybody saw me, all they saw was a flash. By the time I got back to the rink, it was pitch dark, and my team leader was fit to be tied. And that's what I remember the most about London.

By the end of the tour, the late spring of 1988, I'd been away from Edmonton for what seemed like an eternity. No one had seen me since the day I flew to Budapest. When I touched down again, there were plenty of friends and Royal Glenora skaters to welcome me home. At the club, Georges Pinches, the general manager, presented me with personalized licence plates reading "1ST QUAD." I'd barely begun to work with choreographer Kevin Cottam on my new show numbers when it was time to leave again—this time for San Francisco, to start a Tom Collins tour.

That sounds like a mixed drink, so let me explain. Collins is an American businessman who mounts a version of the ISU tour. If the world championships take place in North America, his tour replaces the ISU's. He treats his skaters royally. They stay at the best hotels. The perks and benefits are incredible. If you're a young skater and unused to touring, it's heaven. The problem, in my opinion, is that Collins paid—and still pays—very poorly. He also managed to alienate me forever.

Let's get my side of it on the record and out of the way. A couple of years ago, Collins asked me to do the tour again. I said that I could only do half, because of other personal commitments. We began the negotiations. I needed one day off, so that I could work with my managers in Los Angeles, and proof that the tour had sufficient insurance in case of injury. Money was not the issue. It was never in dispute; we had come to an agreement about that. But I was told by other skaters that Collins said that I thought I could run the tour myself, and that I'd asked for an outrageous sum. Then he told my manager "If you think Browning is going to help me sell one [expletive deleted] ticket in the United States, you're crazy."

I went to the CFSA and refused to do his show again. Unfortunately, many skaters believe that I was being greedy. I wasn't. I don't even want to talk about the shows I in fact did for him.

The rest of the summer of 1988 was a time for reflection and reevaluation. Orser had retired, and, although I hadn't won the championship, I was suddenly ranked number one in Canada. With Orser and Boitano out of the picture, only Petrenko, Filipowski and Bowman were ahead of me in world rankings. Was I supposed to skate differently now? I mulled over the implications and convinced myself that not too much had changed. I still had the same friends, the same skates, the same club to practice at. Most things were going to be the same as before, only a little bigger.

That summer, Kevin Cottam and I began putting together programs for the upcoming season. The 1989 Worlds would take place in Paris, so we planned to make use of music by French composers. We also adopted a somewhat militaristic theme, in keeping with the 200th anniversary of the Revolution.

I flew to Britain in late September for Skate Electric (a new name for the St. Ivel competition). I was late in arriving; I missed my scheduled flight from Edmonton International—because it really left from the Municipal Airport, without me (confusion is my forte). I enjoyed far better luck at the competition, taking the gold medal, followed by Bowman. Filipowski pulled out with a broken skate blade. I also missed my bus to the practice on the day of the free-skating final. It's a miracle I won anything at all!

Three weeks later, I was in Thunder Bay, Ontario, for Skate Canada. I showed up with a cut forehead and explained to the reporters that I'd been in a street fight in Edmonton. Most of them didn't believe me, but it was true. Six unhappy drunks had decided to take a shot at me and Norm Proft, who was training at the Glenora. Push led to shove, which led to a left jab. The jabber wore a ring, which landed between my eyes. Then things cooled down, but Norm and I spent days embellishing our roles as punching bags.

Skate Canada would be my first meeting with Viktor Petrenko since Budapest. He'd placed third there, to my sixth, so I knew a victory or a close second would boost my confidence. As it turned out, he traced the best figures, but I was right behind him. He narrowly won the original program, receiving top marks from five judges to my two, despite the fact that I landed a perfect triple-Axel/double-loop combination. The next night, though, I won the free-skating final, with six 5.8s and a 5.7 for technical merit, and a 5.9, three 5.8s and three 5.7s for artistic impression. Petrenko suffered from wobbly landings on several of his jumps and finished with a 5.8, three 5.7s and three 5.6s for technique; a 5.9, two 5.8s, three 5.7s and a 5.6 for impression. We were inches apart, but I'd beaten the number-one-ranked skater in the world.

The euphoria lasted about a month. In November, at Japan's NHK Trophy meet, I was rudely awakened to the fact that another Soviet skater was still a force to be reckoned with. Alexandr Fadeev had refused to quit after his disappointing Olympics and was back for one last shot at the world title. He'd skated hurt in Calgary, but now he was on the comeback trail. I placed second in the original program, but both Fadeev and Petr Barna beat me in the free-skating final, after I'd botched a triple Axel. Result: Fadeev took the NHK gold medal, Petr placed second, and I had to be satisfied with bronze.

Back at home, the Skid Row brigade had broken up when Ian Ball left to get married. Sunil and I rented another house, in Edmonton's Polish district—a low-crime area until we arrived. While I was at NHK, my Olympic team jacket went absent without leave. Sunil explained that a girl had shown up with two of her friends, claiming she knew me well. The trio fast-talked their way in, then two of them distracted Sunil while the third went rooting through my belongings. He tossed the gate-crashers out but noticed the jacket missing the next day. Fortunately, he knew where one of the culprits worked. He phoned and offered her a choice between a no-questions-asked return and the police. Three weeks later, to my immense relief, the jacket miraculously resurfaced.

That December, I went on a brief show tour in England. Because I'd beaten Petrenko at Skate Canada and Bowman at Skate Electric, the announcers exercised poetic licence by introducing me as the number-one-ranked male skater in the world. It was a touch premature, but I think the memory helped me when I arrived in Paris the next March.

Meanwhile, when the tour ended, I kept my string of airport disasters intact by missing the plane home—fog this time! Standing in the terminal—and not knowing a blessed soul in London—I suddenly remembered that Mom and Dad had met a woman during the Skate Electric meet. They'd bumped into one another at a bus stop outside the arena. She introduced herself as Tina Wilkins, said that she was a great skating fan and offered to guide them around. I'd said hello and goodbye to her, but now the prospect of a friendly face prompted me to phone home (at 2:30 AM, Mom and Dad's time), in search of Tina's number. I threw my things into a locker, caught the subway to her house and visited for hours.

She'd done herself an injustice: she's much more than a fan, she's an authority, an archivist. She had a entire wall full of skating books, tapes and memorabilia. She was showing me film of performances that I'd forgotten. I'm proud to say that she was there in Munich and in Halifax to see me skate.

Two feet of snow and typical February temperatures greeted us in Chicoutimi, Quebec, when we touched down for the 1989 Canadian championships. I was favored to take the vacant senior men's title, while Mike Slipchuk's aim was to re-qualify for the next world competitions.

Slipper and I were one-two after compulsory figures, with Norm Proft, our Royal Glenora club-mate, in third spot. Seeing this, Gord MacAlpine, the CBC radio reporter, nicknamed us "The Three Amigos." Other press members asked us about the possibility of an Edmonton-based sweep. I said that, if we'd known how things were going to turn out, we could have traced the figures back at home. In fact, our showing merely reflected the fact that the Glenora had become the place to be, as far as singles training was concerned.

I sailed through the original and free-skating programs at the Georges Vezina Arena, becoming the first skater to land a quad in Canadian competition. Better yet, it was the best one I'd ever done in public. Slipper took the silver medal, and I placed first, scoring five 5.9s for artistic impression and three for technical merit.

I had plenty of cause for celebration. That night, I became the only skater other than Brian Orser to win a Canadian title at all three age levels—novice, junior and senior. Then, at the closing banquet, I was named team captain for the world championships. We marched around the room, holding the Maple Leaf flag high. Then I invited the eleven other skaters to come with me to the Worlds in Paris and kick butt—a quotable motto that greeted the nation's sports fans with their morning coffee. The one damper on the evening was knowing that we'd have to leave our regular team captain, Doug, at home.

I arrived in Paris in a sky-high frame of mind. My last run-throughs at the Glenora had gone especially well, thanks partly to Cam Medhurst, the Australian champion, who'd been training with us. Cam works harder than anyone I've ever met, in between rounds of mini-golf. Full of life and fun, Cam is one of my best friends.

Paris was in a party mood, ready to celebrate Bastille Day. The Canadian team was booked into a floor of the Pullman-St. Jacques Hotel, a short walk from the Arc de Triomphe and the Champs-Elysées. The Louvre was closed, but I went up the Eiffel Tower with Cindy Landry, the pairs skater. Then we bought bracelets from the street vendors, had our photos taken with two girls from Red Deer, Alberta, who happened to be on their way up, and mimed a skating program for curious passersby.

The next couple of days were spent convincing skeptical teammates that Karen Preston and I were not the love-match of the year. Karen had won the Canadian women's title, and the assumption was that we were having a passionate affair, because we'd camp out in her room till all hours. In fact—for reasons I can't explain—we spent most of the time squirting orange peel into a candle flame to watch the sparks fly, a recreation punctuated by long silences and haphazard debates on the meaning of the cosmos. I've never said skaters are the most normal type of people I've ever met—still, it helped pass the time while our sleep patterns were mixed up by the time changes.

Meanwhile, my sister Dena and her husand Dan Miller had arrived with Mom and Dad. I'd told Dena to save the money, so as to make sure she could be in Halifax the following year, when I thought I'd have a more realistic title chance. But everyone wanted to see how I made out in Paris, and so they'd arrived in force.

Maybe I was inspired by the family presence, but I started thinking seriously for the first time about a first-place finish. After all, I was on a roll—the Budapest quad, the Chicoutimi gold. I'd beaten Petrenko at Skate Canada. Slowly, it dawned on me that I might win this thing, that I should try to go all the way. I talked to Mr. J. about it, and he said, "Of course you should." I didn't know that, behind the scenes, he was guarding against the eventuality of a loss.

The men's singles event of the 78th world championships began on March 14 with compulsory figures. Everything took place at the Palais Omnisports, located in the Bercy district on the south bank of the Seine. This is a unique building, shaped like an Aztec pyramid, with grass growing halfway up the terraced sides. Before the competition started, I made a bet with a Canadian Press staff writer, whose hat—a black fedora—I'd long admired from afar. "Can I have that hat?" I said. "Only if you win gold," he replied. Oddly enough, the hat became a goal in itself, something to shoot for other than the medal, which no one, including the writer, thought I had a prayer of winning.

As you know, figures were in the process of being phased out of world competition and counted for a mere 20 percent of the final mark. I'd placed twelfth in Budapest and worked on them diligently during the winter. I hoped to finish in the top five, which would put me in the elite group who'd skate last in the next day's original program. And I made it— just—winding up in fifth place. Fadeev was first, Petrenko second, Filipowski third and Bowman fourth. But that didn't bother me. I'd got the job done, and I was in a strong position to move up in the original and free-skating programs.

Unknown to me (because the papers were being conveniently lost in transit), the headline writers were having a field day. After my fifth-place finish, the *Edmonton Sun* ran a story that began "The Gold Is Gone." Terrific. Their position had always been that it wasn't there at all. Later, I learned that Mr. J. was the source of many of these stories. He kept giving deep-background briefings to the effect that it would be better if I didn't win, that to peak too early would throw off my timing for a sensible, orderly countdown to the 1992 Olympics. I think he hoped I'd win a medal—probably the bronze—but he didn't believe I could or should take the gold so soon.

I thought differently. My practices for the original program were so-so, but I'd watched Petrenko, and he was obviously not at his best, either. When the day arrived, I felt ready to go. I got to the rink, jogged around listening to the rock group Big Pig on a Walkman and did back-flips in a corridor. Then I watched Slipper skate. He did well, and that was an inspiration.

Mr. J. and I had scheduled a triple-Axel/double-loop combination, figuring that it would be as difficult a jump as the competition's. And so it was. Nevertheless, I landed it cleanly, and then became the first skater ever to land two triple Axels in the same original program. I got seven 5.9s and two 5.8s for required execution, and four 5.9s, four 5.8s and a 5.6 (I still don't know what ailed the West German judge) for presentation. It was enough to earn me first place, with Bowman second, Fadeev third, Barna fourth, Filipowski fifth and Petrenko trailing well behind in sixth. Factoring together the original and the figures, Fadeev remained in first. I was second, with Bowman third, Filipowski fourth, Petrenko fifth and Barna sixth. I drew an early starting position among the last group of skaters for the free-skating final, watched Cindy Landry and Lyndon Johnston win the pairs silver medal and went to bed, thinking, "Tomorrow I'm going to do it. Go to sleep. The future world champion needs his rest."

The next morning's practice was very loose. I glided up and down the ice, talking to Filipowski, then stopped in front of Mr. J., who was trying to tease me by making a huge production of reading a newspaper. "You see," he said, "I have to read a newspaper. You are very boring." I put a touch more energy into my skating, and he put the newspaper down.

After the practice, I went back to the hotel and napped, did some laundry, hung around with Karen Preston, then rode the Métro back to the arena. I was totally relaxed, smiling for no apparent reason. Then, I decided to explore the lower reaches of the sports complex. I wandered around the corridors and found a stairway that led down and down to the innermost core. It was a sort of storage area, filled with machinery, extension ladders and sheets of flooring for the bicycle track. It was a very, very curious feeling—total isolation, complete detachment from what was happening immediately above me. I yelled my head off, jumped up and down and lost all track of time. Maybe the warm-up had begun. Maybe it was over, and I'd missed it! I hurried upstairs, but I'd surfaced too early; it wasn't nearly time. I went outside and sat by a little waterfall, watching the stars, waiting to see whether I'd be world champion. I've been at an awful lot of competitions, and I can remember what I did beforehand at very few, but I remember Paris.

Once our warm-up was underway, everybody was

missing the triple Axel. Then Filipowski landed one, and I applauded. We both laughed, and I went out and did a nice triple-double combination, followed by a less than letter-perfect quad.

When my turn came, I stepped out on the ice, only to learn that Petrenko had received marks in the 5.6 range — certain proof that he hadn't skated well. I shook his hand, loosened up by landing a triple toe-loop, glided over to Mr. J. and said, "If I lose, it's not that bad. I've already accomplished one of my goals for the season. I didn't get a haircut." My hair really was quite long, and Rosemary Marks, our team leader, had been nagging me every day to do something about it. I guess Mr. J. didn't know that, because he was about to run for cover, thinking I'd cracked at last. All I wanted to do was let him know that I wasn't tensed up, that I was ready to enjoy myself.

I loved that final presentation. I hit my quad (it was almost perfect, but I two-footed the landing) and seven triples, including two Axels. Five of the triples were triple-double combinations. Then the marks were posted: seven 5.9s and two 5.8s for technical merit; four 5.9s, two 5.8s and three 5.7s for artistic impression. Bowman skated incredibly, but I held onto first place. Fadeev did poorly. As he left the ice, the reality of the situation began to dawn. Filipowski came on strongly, placing second in the free skate, with Bowman third. The computer mixed and matched the competition's three phases and spat back the final, overall standings. I had won the gold medal, Bowman the silver and Filipowski the bronze.

I was world champion.

What does a world champion do? He goes to the CBC broadcast booth, watches the last three skaters and babbles something that passes for color commentary. I'd never done it before, and I felt too visible. I would have been more comfortable under the stands! Then I walked downstairs, into a corridor beneath the stands, and saw my friend the sportswriter, complete with black fedora. I snatched it off his head and said, "Hot damn! I won the medal, and the hat fits, too!"

I stood on the podium with the medal around my neck, singing "O Canada"—the most fun I've ever had with the anthem. I had to keep an eye on Grzegorz Filipowski, who was hilarious. He was bouncing up and down, waving madly to the crowd. He couldn't believe he'd won the bronze. He kept saying things like, "Can I come and train with you in Edmonton?" "Sure," I said. "You'll feel right at home. I live in a Polish neighborhood."

Then it really started to hit me: I was going to find out what else a champion does. A champion wades through a million interviews, goes to the doping room, then comes back for more interviews. This was spring 1989, and back home the Dubin Inquiry was studying the question of drug use in amateur athletics. The scandal that followed Ben Johnson's disqualification at the Seoul Olympics had cast a pall over the sporting scene, and I was glad to give Canada a chance to cheer again. I offered to strip, to prove I wasn't on steroids. "Figure skaters don't need to bulk up," I said. "I'm proof of that."

During a break in the media circus, I gave Slipper the pin I'd received for finishing first in figures at Chicoutimi as a birthday present; the next day was his twenty-third birthday. There was a party at the hotel, hosted by Barbara Ryan, the CFSA president. I gave my Mom the gold medal to wear and kept ducking into the bedroom to take a barrage of phone calls. Cam Medhurst handed me a bag of Oreo cookies, which I munched when talking long distance with Liz Manley. Then, after exactly two hours of sleep, I was back on the treadmill.

For almost thirty-six hours straight, all I did was run around and talk to people. A telegram arrived from my friends in Edmonton, and I cried over their simple message—the first tears I'd shed since winning. I went to a luncheon hosted by Jane MacLellan and other members of the organizing committee for the 1990 Worlds.

That afternoon, I started to wonder, "What have I done to myself?" Most of my other wins had been very low-key. I was with the team, doing whatever the other skaters did. In Paris, I barely saw my teammates for a day and half. Everything changed, just like that, quick as a snap of the fingers. I woke up one morning, repeating over and over again the phrase I'd heard so many times: *"Champion du monde. Champion du monde."* A skater could get used to that.

But there was still a final day of competition. It featured the women's singles event, and Midori Ito won the gold medal. Watching her win reminded me of our ski adventure in Davos, Switzerland. The previous spring, on the tour following Budapest, she'd wanted to go skiing. The Japanese skating federation was having none of this. Her advisors told her in no uncertain terms that she was to stay off the slopes, or else. So she rode a lift to the top of the run with me and Chris Bowman, looked rather sadly around, then started walking across to the lift again. I called out to her, "Hey, Midori, get on my back." I thought it was a good joke. Midori thought it was an invitation. So there we were, sliding wildly along a slightly sloping roadway. Midori is a tiny person, but skiers aren't supposed to carry a human backpack. Worse yet, I knew that I was toting someone who'd probably be world champion someday. Visions of Japanese lawsuits filled my mind as Midori held on tight, giggling and laughing all the way. Now, a year later in Paris, she was giggling again, and crying tears of joy.

One of the strangest things that happened immediately after Paris was that the reporters were constantly bringing up the subject of my personal life. They seemed to be showing an awful lot of interest in my girlfriends—maybe even more than in my jumps. I wondered if I should write about this at all, and decided that I would, just go get it on the record.

Let me just say, I like girls. If you haven't figured that out by now, you haven't been paying attention. I haven't talked about a lot of girlfriends for several reasons. One: I like to think I'm a gentleman. Two: there weren't all that many. Three: my mom is going to read this book! Four: I'm involved with a wonderful person at the moment, who knows all about my past, but doesn't want to be perceived as "the next in line." She's a big part of my life, but she has a life of her own, as well, and very definite goals. I've tried not to take her for granted, not to assume that, because she makes me happy, she'd necessarily want the world to know.

After Paris, however, I ran into unfamiliar territory. I was at risk of becoming a commodity. There was a big push to market me. We did photo shoots with me wearing cowboy boots. Fine. I grew up wearing them. Then I started to realize that people were saying, "Well, you're certainly going out of your way to present a macho image." That really made me think.

Why was it that some people wanted to make a big deal about my image? I wear the cowboy boots because of my Alberta background, but I also incorporate that image into my performance. I skate in a very aggressive, physical style because that's the kind of person I am—my skating style is part of me. I don't have anything to prove.

8

"CHAMP" OR "CHUMP"— LIFE AT THE TOP

I'd decided after the Calgary Olympics that I had to do something about the business side of my career. After all the financial support that Mom and Dad had provided, it was important that they be involved in my choice of, and dealings with, an agent. Dad and I talked with several people who came on very strong, who seemed to be rather more interested in promoting themselves. After I won the medal in Paris, I was relieved that I'd been smart enough to hook up with Michael Barnett, an agent who knew business and knew me. Everything had been set in place and was ready to roll, on the off-chance that I wound up standing on the podium.

Michael has gone to Los Angeles now. He moved down there when Wayne Gretzky was traded to the Kings, and my day-to-day business is handled here by Kevin Albrecht. But let me tell you one or two things about Michael, who got the whole thing underway.

He was a westerner, raised in Olds, Alberta, not very far from Caroline. I remember the first time he came to the Royal Glenora, shortly after we'd met. We sat around and he said things like, "I do the business and you do the skating. As long as you do the skating right, I'll take care of the rest." Mom and Dad attended that meeting. We didn't commit ourselves to anything. It was all very informative, very educational. Nothing was signed at that point. We decided on a trial run. And we checked him out very carefully; we asked around. Mom and Dad have a real gut feeling for things. They liked and trusted him, which meant a lot.

Mind you, we thought he was a little bit crazy. At one of our very first meetings, he outlined his immediate goals. He talked about the amount of money I'd make, and the fact he thought I was going to win the Worlds the following year. We thought, "All this might be great some day but obviously the man knows nothing about skating, because none of it can possibly happen within a year." But it all happened, exactly as he'd said.

When I won the gold in Paris, an endorsement agreement was made with the Josten's company to have copies made of my world championship ring. I gave them to Dad, Mr. J., my nephew J.J., Wade, Kevin Cottam, Kevin Albrecht and Michael Barnett. It was a great Christmas that year; my shopping was done for me!

Kevin Albrecht

Kurt met Michael Barnett through Brian Stemmle, a World Cup skier and a client of ours. In those days, the firm was known as CorpSport International. It had been formed by Michael in the early 1980s. It was based in Edmonton, and primarily served the marketing and business needs of Wayne Gretzky. Michael had represented Wayne for eight years before he met Kurt. At that time, he represented mostly hockey and football players; he had never shown an interest in a skater before. By 1988 Michael had reached an agreement with Kurt after seeing him at Skate Canada and the Calgary Olympics. Both Michael and Wayne Gretzky saw him there, and Wayne remarked that he was a great athlete with a lot of potential.

Our first task at that time was to get involved on Kurt's behalf with the CFSA, namely David Dore and a gentleman named Bob Howard, a Toronto lawyer, who was then the CFSA's vice-president of marketing. The first year was very unsettled. The CFSA felt that Kurt did not need an agent at that point, that they could look after him themselves. They were dead against him signing with anybody. I think it was largely Kurt's father who thought that Kurt would need someone. He believed that if something was going to happen in the year following Calgary, especially in Paris, it had better be planned for. This showed exceptional foresight. Michael sat down and explained that, if Kurt did well in Paris, the demands on him would suddenly increase. He outlined the basis of a trust fund, speculated as to how much money Kurt might make and explained that he personally believed in Kurt's ability to win.

The CFSA has a central trust fund for all its national

team skaters, capitalized in large part by corporate sponsorships. The money from the fund is then used to pay for training expenses, travel costs, coaching fees and so forth. Thus, while Kurt's parents were entirely responsible for supporting his career in its early stages, he began receiving small amounts of CFSA money when his promise was recognized. After Paris, these amounts increased dramatically, as did his expenses. For the vast majority of skaters the CFSA's system works, but it's not geared to exceptional cases. When it became plain that Kurt was going to prove exceptional, something had to be done.

The ISU rules state that a skater isn't allowed to sign agreements, and that his or her trust fund has to be controlled by the governing body—in this case, the CFSA. But we wanted Kurt and his parents to have input into how the money was invested. So we set up Kurt Browning Enterprises Inc. We wanted to have the money in his trust fund with the CFSA transferred to the company, and keep it in Edmonton. We arranged for an outside trustee named Tom Hamill, Kurt's lawyer. Hamill is a former president of the Royal Glenora Club. He and his partner, John Huckell, went through months of back-and-forth with the CFSA and the ISU on this. It had never been done before; we were breaking new ground.

Now, the major bone of contention, from the CFSA's point of view, was the ISU's amateur status rules. This was our biggest concern also. No one wanted to get their hands on instant wealth, or to flaunt the money in an unseemly way. So we were sensitive to the rules, even though they'd been bent out of shape for years. Many skaters were in fact making all kinds of money, which was put into trust funds. We just wanted Kurt to have some input into the management of his trust fund, and we wanted to abide by the rules. We knew he couldn't actually spend the money, but we wanted him to have some control over the funds from an investment point of view.

Eventually, we put together an agreement for the CFSA's consideration. The CFSA kept trying to block it. They'd had unhappy experiences in the past with agents and felt that it was premature. Kurt hadn't won anything yet. He wasn't even Canadian champion at that time, let alone world champion. The CFSA felt that thinking about business would be a distraction, that he would do better to concentrate on skating. I remember attending the world championships, where the wife of a CFSA board member accosted me. She kept poking her finger in my chest, saying, "Don't—you—take—our—boy—away—from—us." With each word, she'd give me another poke. This was immediately after Paris. These people genuinely believed that outside agitators were going to come in and destroy Kurt. The whole thing was very, very rocky.

In 1990, CorpSport merged with International Management Group, the world's largest sports marketing agency. And now our relationship with the CFSA is outstanding— with Dore, the professional staff, the executive members. We work together; they ask our advice. When we get companies involved with Kurt, which is of course our priority, we'll show these sponsors other CFSA sponsorship opportunities as well. It makes sense for a sponsor to be involved with the team and its events. We put two CFSA board members—David Dore and their president, William Ostapchuk—on the board of Kurt Browning Enterprises Inc. The other members are Dewey Browning—who is the president—and Kurt himself. Kurt's mom, Neva, is secretary-treasurer. But we've never had an issue put to a vote. We have a conference phone call once a year, when we send in the tax return. We have honestly not had a conflict of any kind.

As far as marketing goes, Toshiba Canada's computer and information system division was Kurt's very first sponsorship. They took quite a chance by signing him just before Paris. They were very good to deal with, with the exception of the person who had direct responsibility for the contract. He and Kurt had a serious personality conflict. One day, Kurt said, "I know I'm making money here, but it's not fun. I'm having problems with this guy. I'm not enjoying this at all. Can we get out?" Fun is very much Kurt's bottom line. Nothing gets very far with him if he isn't having a good time. So we ended our relationship with them.

What you have to understand about Kurt is that he makes most of his decisions on gut feel. He is a very straightforward, honest young man who was brought up with values that he can be proud of. He is always thinking about how other people will be affected by his decisions; he has a very humanistic approach to business.

I believe that's why his diet Coke sponsorship has turned out so well. When Kurt thinks of Coca-Cola Canada he can associate faces and names to that relationship. He is not only proud to be associated with the product, but with the people as well. And that's a two-way street, because they then become involved with other projects that are important to him, such as his tours and television specials.

After my Paris gold, the ISU's European tour started in Bordeaux, France. I've already described the joys of touring. This one seemed particularly jangled, because I was dealing with the unaccustomed weight of a world championship. I spent much of the tour in a daze. Somewhere along the line, I was rooming with Petr Barna, in a hotel whose shutters interlocked so tightly that they totally blocked out light. I fell asleep at two in the morning. I put my head down, started to doze off, and then thought, "No.

111

I'll get up and brush my teeth." I'd just finished when Petr started wandering around the room, turning on lights and the TV set. I was trying to get back to sleep like a sensible person. It was two o'clock; I could see the dial right beside me, but there was Barna, pacing around like an idiot. I yelled at him to get back into bed. In reply, he opened the shutters, and light came pouring in. I'd slept for twelve hours without even knowing it. It was two o'clock, all right—two in the afternoon. Ah, Tour Life!

I left the tour early, flying back from London to a hectic round of personal appearances. First was the CFSA's Champions on Ice TV special, which we filmed at Edmonton's Northlands Coliseum. I'd agreed to be national campaign spokesman for the Muscular Dystrophy Association. In June, I flew to Toronto to present a trophy at the NHL awards banquet and play in Wayne Gretzky's CNIB charity softball tournament, where I smashed a grounder between Gordie Howe's legs.

On June 28, the town of Caroline held a night in my honor, organized by Gavin Trimble's mother, Janet, and Reg Dean. That's when they renamed the old arena after me. In July, I was honorary marshall at Edmonton's Klondike Days Parade. Somehow I found time to start working with Kevin Cottam and Mr. J. on new programs for the 1990 Worlds, and I kept in practice at the Royal Glenora. In September, I was back in Toronto, at a luncheon that introduced the commemorative coins for the 1992 Winter Olympics. On good days, I loved the attention, enjoying every minute of my newfound celebrity status. On bad ones, I realized that it was very easy to spread myself thin.

The Champions on Ice tour resumed that fall of 1989. I was glad to be skating alongside Brian Orser once again. He gave me a lucky stuffed animal that he'd been carting around in his skate bag for ten years. Maybe it had a delayed effect, but I can report that good luck isn't immediately transferable.

The trip began promisingly enough. We were in Halifax, and I found myself walking one night with Al Kerslake and Norm Proft, past the Metro Centre, site of the 1990 Worlds. Curious to see what it was like, we found an open door and went inside. As soon as I saw where I'd be defending my title, I walked out to center ice, sat down, gave the matter some thought, and decided that it was a good place, where everything would be fine. If that sounds like dancing for rain, so be it. It psyched me up, and I needed the psyching.

Things started to go off the rails in Indianapolis that October, at the Skate America competition. I had a sore ankle, the result of a tag football game in the park beside my house. The morning of the free skate, I did a triple-Salchow/double-loop—the same combination that had thrown my back out at last year's Canadians. I spent all day in therapy, but nothing stopped the spasms. Mr. J. and I considered pulling out, but I went for it anyway, running on adrenalin. After catching my skate blade in my pant cuff and falling on a triple flip, then two-footing a quad landing, I straggled into third place, well behind Bowman (who landed seven triples) and Petrenko. You can imagine my delight when I arrived home to a stack of newspaper clippings. The *Edmonton Sun*'s headline writers had been at work, announcing that I'd gone from "World Champ to World Chump."

They say that defending is the hardest thing to do in sport, and I agree. That autumn, my entire attitude became defensive. Instead of acting like the good old optimistic Kurt Browning, Go-Get-Em Skater, I started pulling back, trying to give people what I thought they wanted. My reasoning was, "Maybe if I win next month at NHK, the newspapers won't write these things any more. Maybe if I pull off a gold medal, people will believe in me again." I didn't know it, but it wasn't the people who needed to believe in me—it was me.

At NHK—held that year in Kobe, Japan—I fell in the warm-up during a botched triple Axel. Everyone let out a collective "Ohhhh!" sound, and I made a little "Don't Worry" gesture. Then I realized that I'd never have made it if I'd been in a bear-down, truly competitive mode. I wouldn't have loaned my concentration to the audience. If things are going well, and you play to the crowd, that's one thing. If they're going badly, it's not a confident, devil-may-care gesture, it's a cover-up. Not surprisingly, my original program was blown to pieces. I two-footed a landing, opened up a double loop and fell on a triple Axel. My head snapped back and bounced off the ice like a golf ball. I was in seventh place, heading into the free skate, but recovered, scoring enough 5.8s to land me third overall, behind Petrenko (who took first with a raft of 5.9s) and Fadeev.

That year, I was also up against the American skater Erik Larson. He and I didn't get along when we met at Oberstdorf in 1986. I can't explain it; we just weren't on the same wavelength. He'd finished second at Oberstdorf, one place ahead of me. I'd congratulated him; then I declared that he'd never beat me again. This was very unlike me. I was angry—not at myself, or my performance; that happens all the time—but at another skater. It's a waste of energy that would be better applied to the competition. Erik and I get along fine now, and he hasn't beaten me so far—but he very nearly did at this NHK.

Well, it could have been worse. I hadn't won gold, but I took comfort in the fact that I'd been beaten only by a world champion and an Olympic medallist. Back home, I buckled down to work, starting with the Champions on Ice winter season. I tried to think up new and snappy answers to the same question—"What's wrong?"—that was fired at me at every stop, and kept going on the strength of pep talks from Mr. J. "You'd be complaining if they weren't asking you questions," he said. "You're world champion. Answering questions is your responsibility. Learn to deal with it."

So I tried, and I felt much better in December when there were suddenly all kinds of happier answers to give. I came second to Gretzky in a poll conducted among sportswriters and broadcasters to determine Canada's top male athlete of 1989. A few days later, the *Toronto Star*'s Lou Marsh Trophy selection committee had to resort to a tie-breaking second ballot before settling on Wayne as Canadian athlete of the year. Then, just before Christmas, the Order of Canada medals list was released, and I was on it. Unfortunately, the presentations are held in spring or fall, which translates as training or competition. I couldn't make it, they don't deliver, and I still don't have that medal.

9

"Skate God for Life"

It didn't take long for 1990 to start shaping up as the lousiest year on record. Cory Obst and I had been practicing at the Glenora and stayed late to have a goodbye drink with Karen Preston. She had spent some time training at the Glenora and was now heading home to Toronto. We left the club in my car at about one-thirty in the morning and got to within half a block of my house when I hit a patch of ice. My car went out of control and into the nearest hydro pole. Live wires came down around our ears, and a hundred homes lost power for six hours. The officer who administered the breath test—which I'm glad to say I passed—asked for my autograph after the whole ordeal was over.

Then the fun began. My car was kind of hard to miss—a Golf Cabriolet, provided to me by Bob Suitor, the owner of a Volkswagen-Audi dealership. It wasn't in the same league as Mark Messier's Porsche, but with its "1ST QUAD" plates, everybody knew it was mine. An *Edmonton Journal* photographer happened to be passing by the scene of the accident. He'd left his camera at the office, but he phoned the story in. Next morning, I was the hot topic of conversation.

I'm sure some people assumed that I was drunk and was let off easy. The rumor mill was working overtime. A radio host remarked that the real accident would happen when I had to tell Bob Suitor—who stands six-foot four—what I'd done. Actually, Suitor got all sorts of free publicity, gave me another car—same kind, same color—and told me not to worry about it.

Easy for Bob to say. But there's nothing like a burst of notoriety to concentrate the mind. So Mr. J. and I decided it was time to buckle down as never before. I went from being the always-good-for-a-quote world champion skater to an early-morning slogger at the rink. It worked—barely. I had just enough time to pull my act together for the world championships in Halifax. Now, every year, we go through this routine again, getting back to basics before the big meets, like a boxer in last-minute hard training—except that I'm my own sparring partner.

The 1990 Canadian championships in Sudbury were probably my worst competition ever, and I was very lucky to win. About nine or ten days before the meet began, I put on a new pair of skates. The old ones had become too small; my feet had grown or changed. I was in constant discomfort, so we'd ordered a pair that measured half a size longer and three sizes wider. That sounds as if I was flopping around in them, but the actual difference was minute. The boots were fine; it was a relief not to feel pinched and confined. The problem was that I had to match the increase in boot length with proportionately longer blades. They felt all wrong, as if they were sticking out miles in front of my foot. The worst part wasn't the jumps, it was the spins and stroking. I just couldn't get used to them, and I went to Sudbury with a very bad attitude.

Now, you may be thinking, "He had only himself to blame. Why get new skates just before such an important competition?" The answer is, there was an even more important meet—the Halifax 1990 world championships—coming up fast. There was no good time to make the change. But, since it had to be made, then the sooner the better.

Sudbury was an absolute horror show. I wasn't sleeping well. I wasn't skating well. I was snapping at everyone, including Mom and Dad, which is something I never do. I came second in the figures, behind Jeff Partrick, which was all right; I could live with that. I wish I'd won, because this was the final year for compulsory figures at the senior level. But, given the fact that I skated my figures poorly and that Jeff was known for quality figures, I felt content about my second-place finish.

Things really started to go downhill during the original program. Norm Proft came first, with Elvis Stojko second and Slipchuk third. I wobbled into fourth place, feeling sorry for myself. The momentum continued, and the free skate was not my finest hour. I fell on a quad attempt and landed only three clean triple jumps. Elvis was unreal, landing eight triples with ease and grace. For an awful moment, I thought I'd lost the Canadian championship.

The judges were kind to me. It's as if they were saying, "All right, Browning. Here's your title back. Now go home and get settled. Then we'll see what you can do in Halifax." I took first place, followed by Elvis and Slipper, and breathed a sigh of relief.

I remember talking with Elvis about this afterward. We had a rather curious conversation. In retrospect, I guess I was saying to him what Mr. J. could have said to me, before the Paris Worlds. If Elvis had taken the Canadian

118

championship from me in Sudbury—which he very nearly did—it would have screwed up the momentum of his career. He'll probably be champion one day; he's next in line. But in a couple of years, he'll be much more able to deal with the all the stuff that comes with the championship. He won't make my mistakes. He'll learn from them, and handle the pressure in his own way. Right now, his skills are amazing. Technically, he's one of the strongest skaters in the world. But in Sudbury it was his first year in senior, and I told him, from the bottom of my heart, that it was better he hadn't won. I think he understood my motives. I wanted him to believe me when I told him how much I respected him for his skating that day. Afterwards, I felt we were closer as teammates going into the Halifax Worlds.

After Sudbury, I went groping for positive thoughts, bore down in training and worked harder than ever before. At least my skates were coming around, thanks largely to Audi Racz. I'd dealt with him for years and years, starting in Calgary. In those days, the firm was called Professional Skate Service. It was run by Audi's parents. Later, Audi opened a branch in Edmonton. I used to work there for movie money, sharpening, rebuilding and repadding other people's skates. That's how I kept my hand in at leatherwork. Audi's partner, Pat, wanted to specialize in hockey skates, so Audi, who preferred figure skates, opened a new business called National Skate Inc., which is where I get all my equipment today. Audi loves to experiment on the skates. Sometimes I was the guinea pig. Almost always, his experiments worked.

People are curious about my skates. The boots are made by Wifa, an Austrian firm. The factory is very small, so it's not feasible for them to put out a line of Kurt Browning skates—but I'm not going to switch to another manufacturer that could do this. Audi custom-shapes the boots to my feet. By the time he's through, and we've added a pair of MK Gold Star Sheffield steel blades, it's a $1,200 package, not including the hand-carved-by-Kurt-Browning maple leaf in the heel. I told you I enjoyed leatherwork!

While Audi was fine-tuning my skates, I started working on my original program. I'd been struggling with it for months, unable to relax to the music—a combination of Joe Jackson's "Lone Bank Loan Blues," "Toast of the Town" and "Speedway." While in Halifax, all I wanted to do each time I stepped on the ice was to get through it in one piece. The free-skating program—a mix of Offenbach's "Gaieté Parisienne," Massenet's "Le Cid" and a couple of Strauss polkas—was a year old already and up to par, but the original needed all the attention I could give it. After a couple of workouts, I began to find a groove. It took a while.

At a practice in Halifax I fell and cut my thumb during a triple flip. No big deal; I fall more in practice than most skaters. The press was on it like a shot. I was finding out that Halifax was going to be even rougher in terms of media coverage than Paris had been. At least when you're abroad, the international sportswriters content themselves with reporting what they see. Browning falls. Okay, that's our fact for the day. Does it merit a special edition? Of course not; let's go on to other things. But at home—especially when the world championships are taking place on our home turf—everything is magnified. I kept waking up to scare headlines, sensational variations on "The Gold Is Gone." This time, I was floundering all over the ice, I was lost, kiss goodbye to the title forever, and so on.

Then there was the Toller Cranston incident. While I was skating with Stars on Ice this past spring, I told him I was writing a book and asked what he wanted me to say about him. He said, "Don't say you know who I am if you don't really know me." Fair enough—and I confess I don't. He's an enigma; he baffles me. I enjoy his presence because he tells great stories, but he takes a long, long time to tell them. He's very slow, very theatrical. I'm a little wary around him.

The trouble with Toller began just before Halifax. He was doing color commentary for the CBC. Exactly what he said got lost in a blaze of subsequent coverage, but the gist of it was that I hadn't trained, that I displayed a sloppy attitude, and that I was given inflated marks for what amounted to a junior program. He also criticized my appearance—not at the competition itself, but during an early-morning practice session at the Canadians, when I arrived wearing a T-shirt. I think it featured the rock group Motley Crüe. I know that, at some point, he used the word "disgrace."

That upset a lot of people. The rest of Toller's comments were judgment calls. When you're in the broadcast booth, you have to say something. But I've done a little bit of commentary myself. I hope to do more in the future. For me to call a younger skater a disgrace, he'd have to moon the audience. At any rate, all these stories followed us to Halifax. As if I didn't have enough to deal with, everyone was intent on cooking up a Browning-Cranston feud. More than one writer pointed out that Toller was ill equipped to tell a world champion how to behave, because he'd never been one (he had been the world free-skating champion, but had never won overall). My agent, Michael Barnett, was talking about Toller's preference for chiffon blouses. The whole thing was getting out of hand. One day, Toller came over and we had a rather inconclusive talk. He said he didn't mean to slander me, but he didn't exactly apologize. You have to understand that I did not expect an apology; when Toller speaks, there are no gray areas. When the Canadians were over, he'd say that I didn't really deserve to win.

Actually, I found the whole situation very entertaining. I've never held a grudge against Toller. When he speaks up, people listen, because he may be a lot of things, but one thing he isn't is boring! I wish him well.

All of this muddied the waters all week long for the media and the public, but I concentrated on the task at hand. The first stage went better than anyone could have imagined. Halifax was the final world competition to include compulsory figures. I wanted to win them, as a present to Mr. J. I wanted to prove that he could take a misfit jumper and turn him into a figure skater. I came close. Richard Zander placed first, but I was right behind him, followed by Petrenko, Filipowski, Barna and Bowman. Considering that, within living memory, I'd been stuck back in twelfth and fifteenth place, I count that showing as one of my greatest achievements, and a real tribute to Mr. J.'s coaching skills.

The figures gave me an incredible lift, and the entire team was charged up by Isabelle Brasseur and Lloyd (Herbie) Eisler, who won the pairs silver medal. (They'd make it two in a row at Munich, where their chances for gold would have been better if Herbie hadn't hurt his leg playing pickup hockey, which forced him to wear a brace. He and Isabelle are red-hot; a powerful and exciting team. In Halifax, and in Munich, their medals really served to energize us all.)

Now it was time for my original program, and I needed all the energizing I could get. A bad practice had made me uncertain I could pull it off, but once I was underway, my mood improved. I brought off the first combination, then went into a triple Axel and lost concentration. The ten thousand fans in the Metro Center were so noisy I could barely hear my music. On the way into the required triple jump I lost my concentration, and almost the whole jump. I salvaged a sloppy double Axel out of the attempted triple. The next move was a spin. Ever since I was eleven years old, skating in Lacombe, spins have given me too much time to think. This time, I thought, "Well, the triple wasn't great. So what? You landed the double. You still have a clean program." I exited that spin and started another one, busy thinking about trying another triple Axel at the end.

Then, having wrapped up some footwork, I thought, "Wait a minute. Better play it safe. Make that a triple toe."

Almost immediately, I changed my mind. I thought, "No. This mess is your own fault. You're the only one out here. Nobody else can help you. It's got to be the Axel." So I came around a corner in the last seconds of the program, fought for that jump with everything I had and nailed it perfectly. It was one of the happiest moments I've ever had on the ice, because I'd taken it to the limit, hadn't slacked off on a program that I couldn't master all season long.

My marks were through the ceiling. I got a perfect 6.0 for artistic impression, from the Hungarian judge. It was unlikely that Petrenko could match my scores.

And I was right. He didn't match them. He bettered them, with not one, but two 6.0s. He was first in the original program, first overall, and I was second and second.

On the final day of the men's event, Viktor and I rode a bus to the rink together. We were very quiet. In a couple of hours, the championship would be decided for another year, and I'd find out whether I was the first Canadian ever to win back-to-back world men's singles golds. I felt the worst was behind me. The free-skate program was an old favorite, a carry-over (with minimal changes) from Paris. I knew it off by heart. I had a new outfit—a purple job—and even that raised my spirits. I enjoyed the off-ice warm-up listening to Motley Crüe and bouncing around in a back room full of brooms and cleaning equipment.

After my warm-up it was time for the outfit and the skates to go on. The dressing room seemed very quiet and tense compared to the wild dancing that I had going in the back room. When I was lacing up my skates, my thoughts wandered to the Glenora and one of my last runthroughs before the Worlds. That day back home had none of the intensity that this day held. I started joking with the other guys about our outfits—mine was new and loud, while Chris Bowman opted for a tried-and-true black one.

Just then, Mr. J. walked in and asked if I was okay, and I told him everything was fine. As he walked out, he announced that the last skater before our warm-up was on, and I should hurry it up. That got heart rates zooming— we all thought we had more time. Then Viktor said, "I don't think Filipowski has skated yet." He was right, so with one skate on I hobbled out into the hallway to confront Mr. J. I told him that there were two skaters to go, but he insisted that I didn't have that much time left. By the time we'd finished going back and forth on this issue, there was just enough time to get my other skate on.

Tuffy Hough came down to the dressing room to give me a good-luck kiss; we were still dating at that time. She'd arrived with Cindy Landry, who was seeing Chris Bowman. I remember walking toward the ice with Bowman, ready to skate for the ultimate prize, and talking about how good our girlfriends looked. I think our minds should have been on skating.

Petrenko was the first competitor in the final group. I didn't see him skate; I was down under the stands, loosening up, ready as I was ever going to be. When I hit the ice, the four and a half minutes flew by.

I landed seven triples—just one close call. The crowd was on its feet fifteen seconds before the end. A deluge of flowers poured down from the stands. When I made my final circuit of the rink, somebody stuck a yellow fisherman's hat onto my head!

Mr. J. and I watched the marks come up: two 5.8s and seven 5.9s for technical merit; three 5.8s and six 5.9s for artistic impression. Afterward, they showed me Viktor's tally: a 5.6, four 5.7s and four 5.8s on the top row; a 5.7, four 5.8s and four 5.9s on the bottom. He'd skated conservatively, to his cost.

And that, coupled with the marks for figures and original program, was more than enough to nail down my second world gold.

Viktor and I stood on the podium that night with Chris Bowman, who took the bronze with an extraordinary free skate. He knew he'd have to go for broke, so he threw away the script and began to wing it, to the amazement of his coach. When we received our medals, I felt an incredible surge of satisfaction. I'd come through my most difficult season yet, to win a hard-fought battle with two rivals for whom I had nothing but the utmost respect. A little luck and a lot of hard work had paid off. Meanwhile, Mr. J. was busy giving interviews. "When he gets into tough spots, he usually has enough reserves to dig deep down and get out of it, somehow," he said. "In front of a crowd, he's completely at ease. He's a wonderful athlete."

Thank you, Michael. And let's add this: that athlete has a more than wonderful coach.

One of the questions that kept surfacing in my interviews that night was: "Why no quad?" Well, it was there, in the middle of the free skate, disguised as the triple-double combination I turned it into. I went up and instantly knew I didn't have enough height—some other place, some other time."

After the competition, Halifax offered one or two blips on the graph. I remember a press conference involving me, Petrenko and Bowman. Somebody asked Viktor whether the three of us got along. "Oh, yes," he said, through an interpreter, "we have a gay time here." I don't think I've mentioned that Viktor likes girls, too. His English is pretty good, and the instant he'd made this snappy reply, he knew that he'd see it in the next day's headlines.

Then there was the small matter of the "Missing Medal." The night of the awards ceremony, Kevin Albrecht and Dad took it into protective custody and went to a nightclub to celebrate. I was going to meet them there, but after I'd got through with doping, it was too late to run around town. Albrecht, ever helpful, gave the gold to Michael Slipchuk, figuring that he'd catch up with me first. Slipper, ever helpful, decided to brighten up a gathering at someone's hotel, where all and sundry amused themselves by taking pictures of each other wearing the thing. Dawn broke, and Slipper was still playing party animal. I was in a TV studio, explaining to a very dubious interviewer why I didn't know where my second world championship medal had got to.

Later that day, we were back in the arena for the women's final. Jill Trenary, of the United States, was magnificent, fighting off a determined assault by Midori Ito to win gold. Midori was in tenth place after the figures, and most observers counted her out. Moral: never count Midori out. She put on an amazing show in the free skate, jumping—as usual—much too close to the boards. I've tried to warn her off this habit, but she likes to live dangerously. Her choreography puts her right out at the edge of the ice surface; she whirls around the rink like a piece of clothing that's stuck to the outer rim of a washing machine at the end of its spin cycle. (In Munich, when the TV networks had removed a section of the boards to make way for a camera pit, she took a spectacular fall, out through the gap and down amid a gang of startled technicians.) Midori spends her time tempting fate and nursing a crush on Lyndon Johnston, the pairs skater. She calls him "elephanto," because he's about three and a half times her size.

Then we watched the ice dance event, and saw Isabelle and Paul Duchesnay (they're sister and brother) take silver medals. They skate for France, but they grew up in Aylmer, Quebec, and they're tremendous favorites of the Canadian fans. They're completely opposite in temperament. Isabelle is stern and dominating. Paul is shy and extra-polite, quietly passionate. He falls in love at the slightest excuse, but he's constant in his ways. The object of his affection is often a German girl, and he wins them over with the best gorilla-face impression you've ever seen.

The next day, it was time for our exhibition skate. After every meet, the top three competitors in every category come out and cut loose in all directions. People remember this one fondly, and so do I. I did a number Kevin Cottam and I called "The Host," to a Lyle Lovett tune titled "She's Hot To Go." It involves sitting on the boards, making passes at girls in the stands and lip-synching the lyrics. I borrowed Filipowski's hat, which proved to be three sizes too small, and looked ridiculous. Next, I borrowed a CBS camera and started filming Petrenko's number, while another camera filmed me. Then I filmed his interview, the crew and anybody else who popped into my "Kurt-Kam." Everything that had gone wrong all year long went right that afternoon. The whole day was a celebration, a heartfelt sigh of happiness and relief.

The other thing I remember about Halifax is being selected "Skate God." To understand this, you have to understand Scott Hamilton. He won the men's world singles championship four times, capping his career in 1984 with golds at both the Olympics in Sarajevo and the Worlds in Ottawa. I consider skating with him to be a privilege. I could watch him for hours. He's quite small, and his footwork is indescribable. He's a Ninja skater; his feet don't seem to even touch the ice.

He and Brian Orser had a little game they played. When they saw someone do something outstanding, then that person became "Skate God" for the day. When I got off the ice in Halifax, having thrown in the missing triple Axel at the end of my original program to hold onto second place, Hamilton came over and said, "I've just named you Skate God for life." And he wasn't kidding. A year later, during a Stars on Ice tour (built around him, I'll have you know), I did a series of triple combinations. I was catching my breath when Scottie glided by and said, "Skate God for life." The fact that he remembered what had happened in Halifax meant more to me than I can possibly say.

10

BEING FAMOUS

One of the perks and benefits of world championship is that you get invited out more often than might otherwise be the case. In the spring of 1990, I had the chance to attend a concert in Calgary at which Queen Elizabeth would be the guest of honor. When Mom found out that this was in the cards, she informed me that if she wasn't my date for the evening, life as I knew it was over.

My date and I walked into the auditorium and decided that we should sit up top. I was having a marvelous time. I wasn't there with my mom; I was there with a very dear friend. We were laughing and carrying on, in a state of high excitement. We'd just begun talking with some of the people around us when the trumpets played a fanfare. We knew that you're supposed to rise when the Queen enters, so all two thousand of us jumped to our feet. And waited.

When nothing happened, everyone shuffled around for a minute, then slowly sat back down. The trumpets sounded again. Up we sprang—and, after a while, down we went. After three false alarms, it dawned on us that the trumpet section was practicing. That's why, when the Queen actually entered, at least half the audience stayed resolutely in their seats.

When Mom caught sight of the Queen, her eyes lit up. She's not crazy about the royal family, but she's always followed their activities. Some people think it's a waste of time, but there aren't many things to dream about these days, and having a queen is really kind of neat. In any case, I couldn't believe how tiny the Queen looked. She seemed to disappear amid the other people in the procession. People tell me I'm much taller on TV, and that was my reaction to the Queen.

After we'd enjoyed the concert, Mom and I went outside and stood around hobnobbing with people we knew. Suddenly, a rumor spread through the crowd that the Queen was on her way out. I dragged Mom down to the very end of the long, red carpet, where we'd have a clear view. By that time, people had begun to notice me and were shaking my hand or asking for autographs, which didn't escape the attention of a very large man with dark glasses and an earpiece, with a thin wire that disappeared into his suit. "Who are you?" he said. After we got that sorted out, he asked if Mom and I were going to stay where we were. I assured him that my date wouldn't let me go anywhere until the Queen went by. The security agent notified the chief of police, who was by this time coming down the red carpet with Brian Mulroney and the Queen. Occasionally, she'd stop and speak to someone in line; mostly she just nodded or smiled and and moved along. We didn't really think she'd have time to meet us. After all, a woman who wears her jewelry on the outside of her gloves and weights in her dress to keep it down must have lots more important things to think about! Much to our surprise, when she got to us, she stopped, and the Prime Minister introduced me as "our world figure-skating champion."

She acknowledged me right away. I think she said, "I've seen you skate. Congratulations." Mom and I had heard on the radio how you were supposed to talk to the Queen, just in case we got the chance. I knew you couldn't touch her or ask her questions. I was trying to remember whether you could introduce her to people—in particular, my date. But I didn't want to commit a faux pas, so I just said, "Thank you."

"It must be very difficult, what you do," she said.

I didn't want to contradict her, so I said, "Oh, yes. Very difficult." Then, to advance the plot, I added, "But I love to do it." Finally, because we were starting to hit very ... long ... pauses between comments, I said, "Welcome to my home. It's so nice to have you here."

"Thank you very much," she said. Then there was another very ... long ... pause, before she repeated, "So. You love what you do." I thought it was best to agree with that, but I hoped it wouldn't come around for the third time. Then she said that I was very lucky to do something that I loved, and I agreed with that, too. Then she looked at my date, whose hand I was hanging onto for dear life. She nodded, and Mom gave a little bow. All this took maybe thirty seconds or so, which doesn't sound like much, except when you're with the Queen, it seems longer.

Then, for reasons known only to himself, the Prime Minister leaned over and said, "Yep! Taught him everything he knows." The Queen looked totally bewildered by this. I wanted to laugh, but I didn't think it would be acceptable under the circumstances.

After all that, the Queen said goodbye before moving off down the line and into her limousine. I looked at Mom and saw that she'd been eating all this up. Then we were attacked by all the people standing next to us, who thanked us for delaying the Queen so that they could get a good look at her and hear her voice.

There used to be an aerial photograph of the family farm hanging on the wall above the kitchen table. Today, there's a shot of me, Mom, Queen Elizabeth and the Prime Minister, who taught me everything I know.

I was standing in front of a hotel in Hershey, Pennsylvania, when a cab unloaded its passenger—a woman who took one look at me and momentarily lost control. She told me her name was Mary Nelson-Smith, and that she'd come all the way from Montana to see Stars on Ice. I recognized her name; she'd written often. She took my picture and I gave her a kiss. Over the years she's sent me a box of homemade pasta; a song, recorded with her friend Allyson Kellum, called "Must Be Kurt"; and a cookie-cutter in the shape of a steer.

I get rather a lot of fan mail. Some of it comes addressed to the Royal Glenora Club, to the CFSA, to Caroline, to the town of Rocky Mountain House, where I used to skate, or simply to Alberta. "Kurt Browning, Skater, Canada," will get there every time (unlike many people, I'm a big fan of the post office). Dad is really touched by all the letters. I wouldn't have thought he'd be the one to play recording secretary, but it affects him deeply. He feels a connection with the writers; he thinks it's our family's responsibility to make sure they get a reply.

Rosemarie Braun of Bonn, Germany, sent two hundred color photos of the 1991 Munich Worlds. One of my faithful letter-writers, Mrs. V.J. Downing, of East Sussex, England, is eighty years old.

A woman wrote to ask if she could register her dog with my name. (That ought to make waves on the dog-show circuit, when the judges see "Sire: Kurt Browning.")

Sylvia Richter sent small crocheted toys from Germany. Her friend Andrea Fell specializes in picture albums. I've met them both during European show tours. They've become friends of mine. Sylvia and my sister, Dena, are regular pen pals.

Suzy Tetrault of Saint John, New Brunswick, said that I gave her hope "that with a lot of hard work and persistence we can do anything we set our minds to do." Sue Scorizzi of Toronto said she took up ballet lessons because of me. "You are someone who has made a difference in my life," she wrote. "To me, that means a whole lifetime of medals for you."

Why do people write? They're happy for me, proud that a Canadian is doing well. I know exactly what they mean. When Ben Johnson won the gold medal in Seoul, a little bit of it was mine. When he lost it, I lost something, too. When Team Canada beats the Russians, I'm all fired up. I share the Maple Leaf they wear; we're part of the same family. When total strangers write to me, they want to know that they've affected my day, that they've made me think about them by sharing their thoughts with me. It's an exchange—a little something there for both of us. Words on paper are a very simple, very reassuring thing. Writing a letter personalizes me. I'm not some abstract figure in a spotlight. I'm a kid from Caroline, Alberta, a guy who falls down far more often than he does quad jumps, who has a girlfriend, who has good moods and bad, and who worries because he's falling behind in his correspondence.

I don't get to read every letter right away—there are just too many for me to deal with—so Mom and Dena reply with an autographed photo. We go through a lot of those; the last batch of five thousand just ran out. Whenever I get the chance, I'll block off a day or so and catch up on the mail. Believe me, I see all the letters eventually. Every single one is indexed and saved. Years from now, when I'm sitting on the porch and looking back on my career, they're going to spur the most incredible memories. For that alone, I'm in the debt of everyone who's ever taken the trouble to drop me a line.

About 99.5 percent of the mail is honestly motivated and greatly appreciated. Then there's the other stuff. One person took issue with my snakeskin boots. He claimed that they were phony props, and that I was single-handedly responsible for butchering an endangered species. I asked Dad, who'd had them for twenty years, whether this particular snake was on the verge of extinction. He said he didn't think so.

Maybe half a dozen times a year, I get something that's very ugly and a bit frightening—newspaper items with obscene messages scrawled on them, and so forth. These go into the garbage or to the police, depending. There've been requests for money, and the occasional note from someone who's obviously deeply troubled. Anyone who's in the public eye gets his share of these. You learn to deal with them, and you don't have to think about them a lot, because they're few and far between.

Then there's the personal contact with my fans, which I treasure. I could fill an entire chapter just thanking some of the people who've done tremendous things for me over the years, but I'd especially like to mention Keri Pytel and her cousins, Kim and Jennifer Jeffrey. They met me at the airport after Paris, wearing Kurt Browning jerseys. After Halifax, they were there again, with a giant cookie. After Munich, they surpassed themselves by putting me in orbit, through the Edmonton Space and Science Centre's Donate-a-Star program. If you look up in the sky some night, one of those little pinpoints of light is named after me.

That's the good side. The not-so-good side is that, one sunny morning, I was sleeping late, after a small-hours training session. The doorbell woke me up. The bell-ringer said she just happened to be in the neighborhood and decided to drop by. Then she dropped her jacket. I could see she was gorgeous, but I knew that already. I'd met her at the Royal Glenora, with her husband. At times like these, you start thinking very quickly. You wonder: "Is there a photographer hiding behind the tree, ready to capture this moment for the divorce court or tomorrow's papers?" Perhaps you've heard the expression "saved by the bell." My alarm clock went off, and I beat a hasty retreat, shouting "Gotta get to the rink" over my shoulder.

Being recognized wherever I go is pretty standard. If I've just done something notable, it happens non-stop, for about a month, then tapers off. Quite often, there's an element of doubt. People have an image of me as I appear on the ice. In real life, I tend not to be perfectly groomed. I can see them figuring out the probabilities, thinking, "Is it really him?" They don't want to make a mistake. They'd be embarrassed if they accosted some scruffy-looking guy, wearing shorts and a Bon Jovi T-shirt, and he didn't turn out to be autograph material.

Many people want an autograph, but others just want to say hello. I can tell by the way they do this that they think they know me. I'm positive this is what's happening, because I do it, too. If I've seen someone on TV all my life, they're familiar to me, and if I should happen to bump into them, I wouldn't hesitate to start yammering on. Then there are people who go overboard. They say, "Ohmigod! I can't believe you're here. What are you doing at a gas station?" Well, I'm putting gas in my car, so I can drive around. Or I'll be sitting in a McDonald's, and someone will ask, "Where are your bodyguards? Why are you eating chips, all by yourself? Why aren't you off doing something famous?" No easy answer to that one, but it makes me wonder how they think I spend my time.

I should be used to this by now, but I'm always caught a little bit off-guard. When things really got hectic, right after the Munich Worlds, I actually caught myself looking

Left: Sometimes when my world turns upside-down, it's by my own doing! This is one of my favorite parts of being a skater—the fun of giving exhibitions. (Photo courtesy of Andrea Fell.)

Below: Nations Cup 1991, Germany. Kristi Yamaguchi and the American team just barely won the team trophy that day. Karen Preston, Me, Christine Hough, Doug Ladret, Laurie Palmer and Mark Mitchell. (Photo courtesy of Andrea Fell.)

My family is a very large part of my life, and I often look to them for support. Dena, Joelle, Jeremy, Neva, Wade, Jesslyn, Dan, Dewey and some Oiler fan! (Photo courtesy of Randy Heiland.)

Playing charity baseball with Wayne, Janet and Tuffy. Days like this not only help other people, they're some of my favorite memories.

Cynthia Kerluk, Randy Lennon, Monika Schnarre and Craig Simpson. We're all great friends, and when we team up, we help fight muscular dystrophy during the Jerry Lewis telethon.

When I'm off the ice, I like to relax by skating! My nephew Jeremy and I
love to terrorize the bike paths in Edmonton on our Ultrawheels.
(Photo courtesy of Gerry Thomas.)

Sharing this incredible moment with my Mom makes all the years
of hard skating worth every second.
(Photo courtesy of Victor Pilon.)

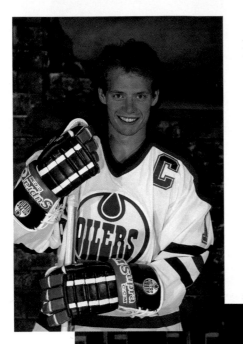

My figure skating has taken me a
lot closer to the NHL and the
CFL than my slapshot or my
punt returns! Here I am posing
with my Oilers apparel as
Honorary Captain.(Photo
courtesy of Gerry Thomas.)

This outfit is from my "Johnny
Guitar" exhibition. Kevin
Cottam and I have put together
some of my favorite numbers.
(Photo courtesy of
Gerry Thomas.)

Skating to "Bring Him Home" from *Les Miserable*s
often brought my emotions out to the ice.
We've received many comments in the mail
from people who felt the same way.
(Photo courtesy of Gerry Thomas.)

Team spirit in an individual sport! Michael Slipchuk
and I celebrate in Munich.
(Photo courtesy of Kevin Albrecht.)

Chatelaine named me one of Canada's "Ten Sexiest Men."
Someone at *Chatelaine* must be a huge skating fan!
(Photo courtesy of David Grey.)

There was an immediate mutual respect between Michael Burgess and I when we met at the Kids' Help Phone, pictured here with Monique and Michael's co-star Susan Cuthridge, after a performance of *Les Miz*.

Just another day in the life of a world champion? The Eskimos firetruck played limosine for John Candy and I at an Eskimos-Argos game.
(Photo courtesy of Walter Tychnowicz.)

Medals, medals, medals! When I see them together,
I can't believe that all my memories of the last three years
can be summed up in just one handful.
(Photo courtesy of Gerry Thomas.)

at people first, to see whether they'd noticed me. If they hadn't, I could relax. If they had, I tensed up. I thought I was committed to them, that I had to behave in a certain way or they'd be disappointed.

All this sounds naive, I know. It's absurd to think that I should be able to walk onto the ice at Northlands Coliseum to get a captain's sweater from Mark Messier, have 17,000 people stand up and clap, and then be able to walk back to my seat without anybody whispering my name. But somewhere, deep inside, that's exactly how I feel. I'm not blasé about the attention, but at a certain level it still comes as a surprise. It takes me a minute to figure out why Michael Burgess, the star of *Les Misérables*, would want my autograph. I've come to see him perform; I'm honored to be in his presence, on his turf. What did I do to deserve his attention? And then I remember. Oh, yeah—I won a medal or two. It's nice that he thinks that's worthwhile.

My family is great about all the time I have to spend just keeping up with my fans and the media and making sure no one is disappointed. Even my young nieces, who love to play with me every chance they get, understand it when my responsibilities call me away and I have to say, "Sorry, I have to go be famous now!"

Someday, I may get Being Famous sorted out, but I've had trouble with it for a long time. I remember when I was very young, going shopping with Mom in Caroline. A lady stopped us and began asking me about my skating— was I doing okay, did I have any competitions coming up and so forth. I'm afraid I was less than gracious. I mumbled something evasive and wandered off. I couldn't understand what business it was of hers. It's not that I was filled with a sense of my own importance, I just considered what I did to be a totally private thing. Mom set me straight on that one pretty quick. She said that, if I chose to skate, I was going to have an audience, people who were genuinely interested in me. If they demonstrated their interest by asking questions, I owed them a courteous and respectful reply. I've never forgotten that day. Now, whenever I've signed one too many autographs, or answered the same question far too many times in a row, I take a deep breath and remember a kid in aisle three of the Caroline supermarket, receiving a valuable lesson from his mom.

The 1990 Tom Collins tour—the last one I'd do—kicked off immediately after Halifax and took me to Los Angeles, where I spent three days with my agent, Michael Barnett, skier Brian Stemmle and the Gretzky household. I took in some nightlife, patrolled the beaches and joined the L.A. Kings' practices, working out under the guidance of defenseman Marty McSorley.

One afternoon, Wayne had to stay behind after the session was over. He gave me a set of car keys and directions to his house. I walked out to the parking lot and found myself the proud driver of a $120,000 limited edition Porsche. Wayne is a very trusting man, knowing my love for speed. The Porsche was a step up from my usual toy—a go-cart at the Warburg track, where Audi Racz, the skate-maker, takes a run at the sound barrier most weekends. I opted for caution on the crowded freeways.

I was very nervous as I drove the car to Gretzky's, but I made it there safely. You can imagine how relieved I was— until I bumped a tire against the curb. I jumped out of the car to check it out. There was a mark on the well that lined up with another mark on the tire—my fault! If it had been my own car, I wouldn't have noticed or cared, but it wasn't my car—it was Wayne's!

When Wayne arrived home, we lined up 1,851 pucks across the living-room floor. He'd just broken Gordie Howe's all-time NHL points record (1,850) and somebody had talked him into scratching 1,851 signatures. Janet joined him on the assembly line while I was assigned to babysit Paulina (who seemed totally unimpressed by the exercise) and two even more unimpressed dogs.

It took me a while—I was really tense—but I finally got up the nerve to tell Wayne about the meeting between his tire and the curb. We went out to inspect the damage, and at first he couldn't even see the mark. When he did, he just passed it off with a wave of his hand, "Don't worry about it." You can believe that my stomach felt just a bit better after that!

If Wayne owed me one for all the babysitting that day, he repaid me in full, because, in a roundbout way, he was responsible for introducing me to Monique Kavelaars.

I was single because that spring Christine Hough and I had broken off our relationship, but not our friendship.

I went to Brantford, for Wayne's annual charity fund-raiser. At a dance one night, Brendan Shanahan, who played for the New Jersey Devils, asked me if I'd like to meet his girlfriend's sister. That sounded promising, because Ingrid is a tall, blond-haired knockout. The dance was a formal; most of the guests were wearing black-tie or ballroom gowns. I looked around and saw a tall, blond-haired knockout, in shorts, T-shirt and ponytail. I thought I was seeing double. Monique and Ingrid are absolutely identical twins.

We only talked for a minute, but she seemed so natural and straightforward that, when she started to walk away, a great big STOP sign flashed in front of me. I asked her what she was doing later, and we agreed to meet at a party, where we danced and talked some more. Then, the next day, we went to Wayne's family's farm for a barbecue and played catch with a softball. When she drove home, I wondered whether I'd see her again.

Two weeks later, I was due to attend yet another charity weekend, this one organized by the Oilers' Craig Simpson in his home town of London, Ontario. And who, I asked myself, was also from London? I called Monique, told her I'd be around and asked if we could get together. We danced all night, traded addresses and kept in touch, which took a bit of doing. During the school year, she lives in Toronto, where she's enrolled in York University's physical education program.

Six months later, having seen each other as often as we could, we decided to keep things going. I'm glad she's around, but she steals my running shoes and sweaters. Also, she competes in the pentathlon, and she's hard to catch.

The May long weekend is very special to me. Another skating season is over, the show tours are finished, and it's time to unwind.

Five years ago, I asked some of my city friends if they'd like to see where I'm from. They knew me only as a transplanted country boy, so I dragged them to Caroline for the weekend. There were eight of us at that inaugural event, down by the lake across from the rodeo grounds, where my grandfather, Jack Browning, started the Big Horn Rodeo in 1933. (I never met the man. He died in a car crash in 1960, six years before I was born.)

By 1990, we'd expanded the guest list to include a larger group, and we introduced an element of danger in the person of Gavin Trimble, who disguised himself as a madman with a chainsaw.

This year, despite Gavin's midnight terrorism, we were back for an encore. Dad and Wade and I pitched three large tents. Others brought their own. The campfire burned nonstop while more than sixty people came and went.

It rained on Friday night, but nobody seemed to mind. We huddled around the fire while Shannon Allison held forth on issues of the day. Slipchuk pitched his tent fifty yards down the road and started a satellite celebration. I was ferrying people to and fro with my nephew Jeremy, and succeeded in blowing the transmission on my long-suffering VW Beetle. Then came the argument: who was driving when it happened? We all combined macaroni, barbecue sauce, mayonnaise and heaven knows what else in a monster pot. This became our staple diet, with Lisa Sargeant's toasted marshmallows on the side.

At 2:00 AM, five intrepid football players decided to scrimmage in the lake. It's shallow enough that no one drowned, but the ball went missing in action.

On Saturday morning, we reassembled at the Lions Club pancake breakfast, featuring the widely acclaimed Dewey Browning as flapjack-flipper. This was a curtain-raiser for the annual Caroline Parade, which winds its way slowly down the main street; luckily, this being Caroline, we didn't have to worry about stoplights! I was on the senior citizens float, along with J.J. and Al Kerslake, who had arrived from Guelph just in time to climb aboard. I don't think anybody minded our hitching a ride.

Lady, a dog belonging to the Goodmans, wore a red bandana around her neck and was supposed to lead the parade, but she deserted after only a single block.

Entries included a tow truck towing another tow truck. The one in back belonged to the loser of a Stanley Cup bet. Several people rode horses. The beauty salon's float featured three kids dressed up as The Simpsons. The Caroline School band played "When the Saints Go Marching In." The fire truck and the ambulance did their best to drown this out with blaring sirens. Everyone was careful to uphold a time-honored Caroline tradition by throwing candies to people on the sidewalks. The McQuiston Plumbing and Heating van—uncompromisingly undecorated—brought up the rear of the procession.

When the festivities ended, it was time to adjourn to the Caroline Hotel's Sportsmans Inn, where a country-and-western duo entertained. Curious city friends took turns sipping at a mixed drink created in my honor when I landed the Budapest quad—a blend of four lethal ingredients, guaranteed to make anybody turn around four times and then fall down.

Back at the lake, a rodeo was underway, with chuck-wagon races followed by a barn dance in a real barn with real straw on the floor.

On Sunday afternoon, we descended on the softball diamond for a long-awaited grudge match between the Browning Family Team and the Thin-Ice Skaters (starting pitchers Dena B. and Matthew Williams). Torn between two loyalties, but wanting to be on the winning side—the trophy, a cow's skull, was much desired by all—I stuck with the Brownings. To my dismay, the skaters scored a fast two runs in the seventh and final inning to squeeze out a victory. Fortunately, Commissioner Dewey Browning noticed three skaters sitting in lawn chairs in the outfield—an unorthodox and clearly illegal move, since the maximum number of outfielders who can sit in lawn chairs during any one inning is two. The skull therefore reverted to its rightful place, back at the Browning homestead.

By Monday afternoon, the last stragglers had finished cleaning up the campsite, and I said goodbye to Al Kerslake.

"Only 360 more days till the next long weekend," he said.

"Can't wait," I replied.

The summer of 1990 called for a number of decisions. First, I had to come up with a new free-skating program, aided by a new choreographer, Brian Power. Kevin Cottam had helped me design the programs that secured us two world championships, but I felt the need for a change. I think it's important to take fresh directions and listen to different ideas, right down to the design of my skating outfits. Mom did all the sewing before I moved to Edmonton; then Vicki Clydsdale took over, creating the costumes for the 1987 and 1988 Worlds. Ever since Paris, wardrobe has been the responsibility of Allison Yardley Jones, except in 1990, when Mr. J. suggested that I have the Halifax free-skate outfit produced by the seamstresses of the Toronto Ballet. That one cost more than $1,200. Usually, the price tag is more like $500—a bargain, considering the weeks and weeks of work.

I also had to find time for Don Metz, who was producing a videotape titled "Jump." It was sort of "This Is Kurt Browning's Life." It included everything from interviews with my parents and friends to all my favorite performances at the Worlds. If that wasn't enough to keep me busy, I spent a couple of weeks moving out of the house I'd been sharing with Sunil and into a place of my very own—in between practicing for Ted Turner's Goodwill Games, which were scheduled to take place in Tacoma, Washington, in August. I hadn't planned on going, until I heard that both Petrenko and Bowman would be there; I changed my plans immediately.

The Goodwill Games were a very unusual experience, more like the Olympics than a skating competition. Athletes of every kind were in attendance, from basketball and baseball players to track-and-field stars like American sprinter Carl Lewis. It was hard to concentrate on my brand new programs, which I usually wouldn't have bolted down until October or November. This year, though, with the elimination of compulsory figures, they'd assumed an even greater importance, and I was glad to get a head start on mastering them. Brian Power had suggested a serious theme for the original program—a radical departure from my usual lighthearted numbers. I was delighted when both my programs were well received by the audience. And by the judges, too. Despite strong showings by Chris and Viktor, I returned to Edmonton with yet another gold.

Almost before I turned around, the autumn competitions were underway. First on the list was Skate Canada, held that year in Lethbridge, Alberta. Only one other top-ranked competitor—the number-four-rated Filipowski—was entered. I continued to experiment with my choreography, and I must have been a trifle off during the original program, which Filipowski very narrowly won. Actually, this program was one of my best ever until the double Axel landing, which I over-rotated. I was very upset afterwards because I had a feeling that with that small mistake I had given up an assured 6.0. But I came back to beat Filipowski in the free skate and take the gold medal, receiving a 5.9, two 5.8s and four 5.7s for artistic impression.

Meanwhile, Petrenko had not been idle, winning the Skate America meet in Buffalo, New York. He too was introducing new programs, and they were shaping up sensationally. He landed two triple Axels in his free skate. Everything I heard indicated that Munich was going to be very interesting indeed.

My next stop, in mid-November, was Gelsenkirchen, West Germany, for the Nations Cup. I won the original segment, scoring in the 5.5 to 5.8 range—a little off, because I'd twisted my knee in practice. Todd Eldredge skated before me in the free skate and drew a string of 5.6s to 5.8s, which charged me up. These marks may sound a little low, but the quality of his skating that day was superb. I landed two triple-triple combinations, including a triple-Salchow/triple-loop—the first ever completed in competition. Despite falling on a triple Axel, I took gold again, receiving marks between 5.6 and 5.9.

Back in Edmonton, I lost three weeks of practice time when we launched into filming for "Tall in the Saddle," an hour-long TV special for John Brunton's Insight Productions. I'd been looking forward to this because Brunton, the director Joan Tosoni and their entire team were willing to listen to me from the very first. Considering how many cooks wind up stirring the television pot, it was amazing how many of my ideas made it through to the final product.

I had three choreographers this time around: Cottam, Olympic teammate and friend Rob McCall and Sandra Bezic, who I hadn't worked with for ages. Slipper and Norm Proft were on hand for our legendary "Three Amigos" segment, and I skated pairs with Kristi Yamaguchi, who'd moved up from the States to train at the Royal Glenora. My other guest was Gary Beacom, who did the most fantastic numbers imaginable. He's on the professional circuit now, which I think is just fine—it means I don't have to skate against him. He's always gone his own way; he should have every skater's admiration and respect.

I've talked about balmy Alberta weather, but it failed to materialize that December. I'll never forget trying to finish off a triple loop out on a frozen lake. Brunton had hired some inmates from a nearby correctional institute as snow-shovelers. He thought it would make a nice change of pace for them, but after about an hour, they wished that they were back in their cells. The wind-chill factor brought the temperature to forty below zero. I kept getting blown off-balance and had to do that miserable jump fourteen times, wearing only a Western shirt. It was so cold that my blades wouldn't melt the ice. Usually, the weight of your body and the friction of the blades will melt the top layer as you go along. But on ice that hasn't been flooded—that's just been sitting there for weeks getting colder and harder—you feel as if you're skating on sand. My blades made a wild, squeaking sound, like fingernails on a chalkboard. Occasionally, the ice would crack, and men with blow-torches rushed around, trying to patch it up.

Things were even colder at Em-Te Town, a western village just outside Edmonton. This was where Slipper, Proft and I got done up in chaps and ten-gallon hats for our famous cowboy turn, and Beacom played a satanic fur trapper. Still, it was a relief to get back inside the Caroline Arena. We started the shooting with a full-capacity audience, and I can't thank those people enough for acting as extras, watching Kristi and me do the same number again and again. Then a storm started to blow, and some of them had to leave, to drive back to other towns. Those who stayed allowed themselves to be herded around the rink, to make it appear as if we were playing to a standing-room-only crowd.

Just as filming was about to end, I received two unexpected pre-Christmas presents. First, I was notified that I'd become the first figure skater ever to be selected by the Canadian Press as the recipient of its Lionel Conacher Award as Canadian male athlete of 1990, finishing ahead of Mark Messier and Gretzky. Then, to top it off, the *Toronto Star* called two days later to tell me that I'd won the Lou Marsh Trophy as Canada's athlete of the year.

The Christmas–New Year's holiday allowed me to recover from both the shock of these awards and a bad case of flu, a result of that "Tall in the Saddle" shoot. I played with my nieces, hung out with Monique (who'd flown in from Toronto) and thought about my competitive programs.

I found I was hungry to skate, which Mr. J. appreciated. He'd been fretting all through my absence from the rink. I'd fallen behind in my lessons, which may have accounted for his foul humor at the divisional meet in Yorkton, Saskatchewan. I missed a combination jump (actually, I didn't even attempt it), and when I came off, he exploded. He said I'd been pulling out of triple Axels all week. I said I hadn't, and away we went. Finally, he shouted, "You are full of shit! No, wait! You are full of chicken shit!" I started to laugh, which made him even angrier. Luckily, we got back on an even keel in time for the next day's free skate, which was one of my best. I now felt I was ready for the Canadians in Saskatoon.

It was February, but Saskatchewan was going through its version of a chinook. In keeping with the weather, I had a red-hot practice—three clean quads, a couple of triple Lutzes and several triple combinations. Then my back went haywire. It was a replay from Skate America in 1989, and the spasms were painful and intense. Mr. J. and I considered withdrawing from the competition. The next day, after a session with Bruce Craven, the physiotherapist, I felt somewhat better, but Friday afternoon, when I walked into the practice rink, I wasn't sure whether I could defend my Canadian title with an original program that night.

Word had spread, and a battery of reporters was awaiting our decision. I tried some jumps and huddled with Mr. J. I felt all right, so we thought that we'd go for it. A fortunate choice—I was first in the standings (receiving my only perfect 6.0 at a Canadian championship) and first in line at Bruce Craven's door afterward. But I wasn't in the clear, by any means. Elvis Stojko was on my heels again, just as he'd been the previous year, in Sudbury.

And, for the second year running, my performance in the free skate was nothing to cheer about. I two-footed the landing on a quad, completed only four triples, stumbled on a triple-triple combination and fell on a triple Axel. Elvis landed six triples and received higher technical marks—5.8s to my 5.6s. I won my third straight Canadian championship. Again, as in Sudbury, this one was won on artistic impression: a 5.9, five 5.8s and a 5.7, while Elvis managed only 5.4s to 5.6s.

As for the rest of my friends, Slipper cruised safely into third place, making sure we'd be together on the world team again. Josée Chouinard edged Lisa Sargeant for the women's title, Brasseur and Eisler took pairs, while Martin Smith and Michelle McDonald won ice dance. We were sad that Karen Preston wouldn't be with us, but happy for Josée Chouinard. She has a touch of Liz Manley's spunk and personality; she'll be very big, very soon. In Saskatoon, she'd just begun to climb aboard the world-team express. The next month, in Toronto, Kevin Albrecht and I picked her up at six in the morning, en route to the "Canada A.M." studios for an interview. She crawled into the back seat, three-quarters asleep, and started mumbling about the inhuman hour. I looked at her and smiled, and said, "Welcome to Hollywood, kid."

An NBC film crew arrived in Edmonton in February to prepare a profile on me before I left for the Munich Worlds.

They'd already been to the Soviet union, to Odessa, and filmed Petrenko. I hadn't seen that footage, of course, but I had a pretty fair idea of what they were up to. They wanted me to go to a bar and dance and drink beer for the cameras. Finally, we settled on a brief sequence that involved my shooting pool.

The end result, when it aired, fulfilled my expectations. They'd made it appear that everything north of the forty-ninth parallel had been corralled by Kurt Browning, while Viktor couldn't leave his house to have a sandwich. Our training styles looked like an outtake from a *Rocky* film. Viktor grimly lifted weights, did sit-ups or struggled with an exercise machine, while I played tennis. "The cerebral Petrenko" was shown in a bookstore, as opposed to "the commercial Kurt Browning," whose hard-sell image was plastered everywhere. To support these conclusions, the crew filmed an hour-long interview that yielded about two minutes of air time. There were all sorts of questions about money; they'd definitely settled on the wild young playboy with a condo full of party girls versus the penniless little Soviet who walks along the Black Sea contemplating life. Then they filmed me skating through clouds of dry ice, as if the entire project wasn't foggy enough already.

And there went another day's practice time. I wasted a bit more energy by getting angry, kicking holes in the ice and complaining bitterly to Mr. J. about the swarms of TV cameras. He managed to frighten most of them away long enough for me to get some real work done. When the cameras were gone, I settled into some great training weeks. I wish I could always skate that well. I was enjoying the practices and the way my body was reacting to the heavy training.

The media attention was compounded by a comment I'd made after the competition in Saskatoon. Someone asked me if I was going to retire after the Albertville

Olympics, and I said, "Yeah, sure. Probably." Result—a burst of headlines stating "Browning will retire."

An especially bright spot in those jangled two weeks was my third consecutive Southam Award, presented by Marty Knack of the *Edmonton Journal* to Alberta's amateur male and female athletes of the year. Marty is a self-educated expert on my sport. He takes his coverage very seriously and follows skaters even before they've won a competition. (Not to mention that he lets me win at golf!) The fact that my back muscle seemed to be under control again and Mr. J.'s comment that I was skating more consistently, more maturely than usual fueled my confidence. I knew I was improving, feeling stronger every day, and ready as I'd ever be for Munich.

11

"MEDALS, MEDALS, MEDALS!"

Nobody in the world can give a massage like Alex Pogrebin-ski. Just before every major competition, I visit him at the Royal Glenora and place myself in his hands. First, he takes a bunch of oak leaves, tied together like a brush, that he's soaked in soap for a couple of weeks and brings them into the steam room. Then he brews up some lemon tea, laced with what I think is brandy but may be a mystery substance of his own devising. When I've digested it, I lie down with a wet towel over my head and Alex goes to work, softening me up with the soggy foliage and rearranging my muscles one by one. Brian Orser used to be a devotee of rolfing, which always sounded to me like a cross between deep massage and drilling for oil. But Alex is a Russian wizard—a sports therapist who can turn you around with a touch of his fingers. I go to see him on the slightest excuse; he makes the pain go away.

Thanks to Alex's ministrations, I took off for Munich and the 1991 Worlds in an optimistic glow, flying from Edmonton with Mr. and Mrs. J., their son (Alex) and Lisa Sargeant. We touched down in London, only to learn that the travel agency through which we'd booked our tickets had gone bankrupt. So much for the connecting flight to Munich.

Stranded at Heathrow, we shopped, read books, napped on a bench and played with a pocket calculator. During the flight, we'd used it to estimate that, by the time the 1992 Worlds rolled around, I'd have done 1,300 triple Axels. Not content with this useful information, we buckled down to serious number-crunching and decided that, on the night of the free-skate program in Munich—if we ever got there—I would be exactly 10,000 days old. Six hours later, we were rescued by Canadian Airlines and caught a plane to Germany.

Our entire team had been booked into the Sheraton Hotel, just northeast of the central Marienplatz. We had a floor to ourselves, with security guards posted at the elevators. A spare room was designated as the lounge, where we passed the time with a scrapbook of collages made by tearing out photographs from European magazines and superimposing the faces of our favorite judges and teammates. A country and western singer wound up with Elvis Stojko's head, and there were several highly imaginative groupings of fellow skaters in compromising positions.

I roomed with Doug Ladret, because Slipchuk wanted to team up with Martin Smith, who skated in the dance event with Michelle McDonald. Martin and Slipper are a two-man demolition crew, so Ladret and I left them to amuse themselves while we settled for peace and quiet. Doug spent his spare time tie-dying shirts with a world championship design, which he sold for twenty-five dollars apiece. The proceeds went toward team expenses, and everyone's parents bought one. Unfortunately, Ladret hung his handiwork in the shower to dry. Every time I tried to bathe, I had to thrash my way past a rack of soggy souvenirs.

The first two nights in Munich, I slept like a baby. The third, I went to bed at midnight, woke up at two o'clock and couldn't get back to sleep. I went to the team room, so as not to bother Doug, made phone calls home, watched rock videos on TV and glued some more pictures into the team book, then headed straight for 7:00 AM practice, feeling confident and relaxed.

Munich was the first Worlds to eliminate compulsory figures. This meant that competition began the following day with our original programs. It also meant that we needed some sort of mechanism to determine skating order. Previously, we'd skated according to our showing in the figures. The top five (sometimes the top seven) entrants skated their original programs last, one after the other. This made it easier for the judges to compare their performances. But, if you'd done poorly in figures and were trying to catch up, you might be buried in the middle of a mob of skaters and escape the judges' notice. In future, I wouldn't mind switching to a seeding system, as in tennis. That would ensure that the skaters who are likely to skate the best, based on past performance, are grouped head-to-head, instead of scattered throughout the field. But no such luck in Munich. Our starting order was determined by purely random draw, and I drew a spot in the middle of a pack of thirty-four. It could have been worse; I didn't want to skate first under any circumstances.

The day before the competition was to begin, we had a practice, and it was incredible. Elvis Stojko and I were on the ice together. Both of us had finished the important elements of our programs, and we decided to have some fun and try side-by-side quads. I landed mine, but Elvis stepped out of his landing. When we went over to our coaches, Mr. J. called Elvis over. Elvis thought he was in trouble, but Mr. J. just wanted to poke some fun at him: "Don't let Kurt sucker you out." Elvis rose to the occasion with a quad-toe/double-toe combination, then bowed to all points of the compass.

By this time, people were starting to pay attention. Enter Peter Jensen, who shouted to Elvis, "Do your impersonation!" Elvis shuffled around for a second, then began an absolutely devastating take-off of my skating style. He stamped his feet like an angry bull and struck my opening pose, holding it so long that it became ridiculous. Then he was off, waving his arms like a windmill, punching the air with super-dramatic and super-speedy movements, bouncing all over the ice. I thought he was my evil twin, let loose to haunt me. Obviously, he'd been working on this for quite a while, because he sure was accurate. But I wasn't going to let him get away with it unchallenged. I hadn't prepared a parody of his style, so I skated out beside him, and we started to play me-and-my-shadow, gliding down the ice in tandem like a couple of dolphins at Marineland. I did a quad-toe/triple-toe combo, but had to reach down and touch the surface with my hand. Then I did a triple-axel/triple-loop. The crowd was in an uproar, and the announcer came on the public address system, saying, "Unfortunately for our viewing audience, there are only three minutes of practice time remaining." I tell you, Elvis is amazing—a jumping machine. He's going to be very, very big; his time is coming.

After the practice, it was time to start counting down to the next day's original programs. I was eager to get out there because my presentation represented something completely new. I was cast as a Hindu war god, whose arms—all six of them—made elaborate and symbolic movements. This was the character that Elvis was lampooning; he certainly had a lot to work with. The choreography was done

151

by Brian Power, who explained to me that the god—a composite of Siva and a couple of other deities—was fierce and majestic. One hand motion might suggest an elephant's trunk; another, a beating drum or a raging fire. I don't want to mislead you here—I didn't have six artificial arms or an ornate headdress. The costume was actually very restrained, considering that, at the Canadians, I had a silver snake running down my leg, with his head on my boot—when I spun, he looked like a barber pole. The war god's costume was dramatic enough for anyone's taste but relied more on subtle effects. I had a silver top, with a metallic sheen, like armor. The pants were flowing, almost like harem pants. I also wore a wide leather belt, a leather breastplate and a matching wristband.

During this number, I skated to music by Borodin and Mozart, intercut with a segment of Phil Collins' "Find A Way To My Heart." That sounds eclectic, to say the least. Let me tell you how this came about. Brian Power wanted a very brief passage to suggest one of the war god's activities. Brian called it "The Churning of the Universe." He was going crazy trying to describe what he had in mind—sort of an "Ommmm" sound, more like a sound effect than music. The image was something vast and primal revolving in outer space. Brian couldn't find anything that suited him and was about to resort to a synthesizer. One day, he was sitting at my house, and I happened to put on a Phil Collins album. Suddenly, the sound that Brian had been struggling to put into words came thundering out of the speakers, complete with an insistent drumbeat. Brian came thundering down the stairs, shouting, "What's that? That's exactly it!" All in all, what we'd put together for Munich was strong, unusual music that would help reflect a growth and a maturity in my skating, something to put distance between me and the brash young characters I'd played in previous years.

Viktor Petrenko had drawn a position in the group that skated before mine for his original program presentation.

Elvis and I were in the same group, so we arrived for our warm-up together, checked into the dressing room, then began wandering around the rink, testing the atmosphere and adjusting our eyes to the television lights. As we were signing autographs, Petrenko began to skate, and I watched him for a few seconds until Mr. J. very politely told me to get lost. "You have enough to think about," he said. "Go somewhere else until he's finished." I realized that Mr. J. was right. I also realized why I was hanging around. Because of the random draw, this was one of the few times Viktor and I hadn't been grouped together.

So there I was, skates on and ready to go, with plenty of time to kill. I found an empty dressing room, ran myself a drink of water and sat down to wait. I think I even closed my eyes for a second. When I opened them, I was surprised to see Chris Bowman's mother, visibly nervous for her son and in search of a place to hide. We looked at each other and laughed. Then, clear as a bell and twice as loud, I heard Viktor's marks being announced on the p.a. system. Since I'd hidden myself away to avoid hearing them, I thought I might as well get silly. I stuck my fingers in my ears and started whistling and humming, repeating nonsense lyrics along the lines of: "Yum dee dee, not listening to Viktor's marks, sitting and wasting time." And so on. You can imagine the effect this had on Bowman's mother. Worse yet, I unplugged my ears too early. All I heard was: "5.8, 5.9." Great. Viktor had skated clean and well. The 5.9 suggested better than well. I'd done all this silly mumbling and chanting for nothing, but I couldn't stop now, so I stuck my fingers back in my ears and made up another lyric, until Mrs. Bowman looked at me and said, "He's finished now. You can stop that." At least I think that's what she said, because I was reading her lips.

Suddenly, stuck there in a dressing room with Christopher Bowman's mother—and having just learned that Petrenko was going to make life difficult for me yet again—I started thinking about her son. I used to think he was unbeatable. He's very striking, very large and muscular. But he has an oddly expressive, almost childlike face. He lands a jump and gets a sort of I-Know-Something-You-Don't-Know look. He flashes you the big grin; he knows how good he is, that he's not going to go down in flames. Audiences love this. Whether you like what he's doing or not, you're going to watch him skate.

In Cincinnati, Bowman was third in the free-skating final, right behind Orser and Boitano. Many people would say he skated better than either of them. He had so much finesse, so much personality. He seemed to love life more than he loved skating. Nothing wrong with that; he lived it to the hilt. Then, when he refocused his energies on skating, it presented a challenge. It's almost as if skating in and of itself was too simple for him. He was so good, it bored him.

I never really got on the same wavelength with him, and there were times when the whole thing got uneasy. He used to call me "The Marlboro Man," because of all the cowboy press, and I didn't know how serious he was, so I got quoted to the effect that he was from another planet. But he's worth talking about—and he was worth thinking about that day—because he's so interesting. That week, though, he was keeping pretty much to himself. So I wished him luck through his mother and walked up to the ice.

The warm-up went quickly, and I was out and skating my original program in no time flat. I felt on top of things and very confident—much more comfortable than the previous year in Halifax. I was moving quickly, feeling every move and thinking things like, "I've only got four crossovers before I turn around, so I have to make sure each one is strong." It's important that my first steps are secure and that I'm seen to enjoy doing them; the judges pick up on that.

I skated by the end of the rink, past Kristi Yamaguchi's seat. I very nearly looked at her, but then I thought, "No.

Keep your mind on what you're doing. If you look at her, she'll think you're losing concentration, and it will scare her." So I skated by, looking straight ahead, and went into a triple-Axel/triple-toe combination. I'd landed it perfectly in practice again and again, but I'd had trouble with it everywhere else—at Skate Canada, the Goodwill Games and the Canadians. This time, I was mentally prepared. The key was to do it exactly as I'd done it at the Glenora: no more emphasis and no less; no rush but not a second's delay. I went up and landed and went up again. In midair, I thought I'd waited too long to start rotation, but I hit it. Then I told myself, "Hold the landing," and it worked to perfection.

The next move was a death drop. (I know this sounds fairly blood-curdling. Actually it's a spin that looks as if I'm going to tumble face-down.) I did it almost instinctively. Halfway through it, I had to remind myself that it was just as important as the combo. "Every element, one at a time," I thought. Then I skated around a corner, made sure I had sufficient room and went into my triple-flip. Suddenly, a new thought flashed through my head: "You're at the Worlds, and this really, really counts." I was momentarily distracted; I let the situation take over instead of the training. I hit the ice under less than ideal control, but the jump was clean, and that was all that mattered.

Now the hardest elements were behind me, and I could relax a little. I wanted my next moves, the circular footwork, to be strong and fast, getting faster as I moved around. Halfway through, my choreography called for the Hindu war god—who was nothing if not multitalented—to play an imaginary flute. I decided to improvise, based on a conversation I'd had earlier that day with Tuffy and Doug. Tuffy said she couldn't attend the program, but that she'd watch it on TV. We joked about the flute-playing, which comes at a point where I'm sometimes off-balance, and I said it would serve me right if I slipped and stuck my thumb in my mouth. So, at a point on the ice where the judges couldn't see me, that's exactly what I did. I smiled to myself, wondering how Tuffy and Doug would react seeing it on TV!

The next spin was a difficult one that involved lifting my knee up high. It always gave me trouble—I've never been a fan of spins—but I got through it safely, with no points lost. After that, my mind began to wander again. I spent the next couple of moves wondering if the program was as good as it could have been. And then, with a double Axel and a final spin, I was finished. I stopped skating, and I could feel myself trying to stay in character. I'd laughed and smiled during the program, but now I felt it my duty to the war god to be brisk and businesslike. I took my bow— maybe a little stiffly—and skated over to Mr. J., my arms full of flowers that were handed to me or thrown on the ice. I felt satisfied I'd done my best—aside from a slight wobble on the flip—and fairly certain I'd won. I stood there and watched the first few 5.8s and 5.9s go up, assuming that they'd push me past Viktor's scores.

Trying to figure out judging is the most frustrating exercise imaginable. I didn't really respect or care about judges until I started traveling to international events. Then, all of a sudden, they weren't merely names at the top of the marking sheet. They had personalities and emotions, husbands and wives, kids and a mortgage to pay. It was like getting to know one of your teachers in grade school, finding out that Mrs. Smith is a real person with a real life. When I began to travel with them, saw them at breakfast in the morning, sitting nervously all day long, staying up late at night writing letters to a referee to justify their marks or explain a mistake, I became a touch more sympathetic.

I don't know how many times a judge has come to me and said, "Make my job easy. Get on the ice and do what you can do." So that's exactly what every skater attempts.

Judges will naturally want their country's skaters to give them a valid reason to assign high marks. If you skate well, they can in good conscience score you well, it's as simple as that. And you must skate well always. The judges are there at practices. They can't evaluate thirty-odd guys the first and only time they see them so they watch you constantly. They take notes throughout the week. Also, as I've said, they keep track of your record at various competitions throughout the year. The image lingers. You must be aware of this.

Yes, judges make mistakes. It's called being human. But glaring errors are few and far between. Once, a judge looked down to make a note and missed an element in a skater's original program. The jump was done, no question about it. But she didn't see it. Up go the marks, and she's .5 lower than everybody else. Having figured out what she'd done, she then marked everybody else .5 lower on everything for the rest of the day. She put herself in a difficult position and probably confused the audience with her reactions. It wasn't the most reasonable thing to do, but it must have seemed like a good idea at the time.

It's fatal to make assumptions about judges, to think that they'll automatically mark you in a certain way. I've heard skaters say things like, "I know I've got the Polish judge." That's nonsense. All it can possibly mean is that the Polish judge is ready to give that skater top place if he earns it. You have to prove you can do it. The rules are different here. It's not showtime. I have to impress these very hard-nosed people who've seen it all. They aren't biased, but they do have expectations. I'm slotted before I even step on the ice—a defending world champion. That carries a lot of baggage, both good and bad. In Munich, I wondered if it counted for or against me.

But at that particular moment, it didn't matter why Petrenko was ahead of the game, only that he was. And I'd have to do something about it. For the third year running, I would have to move from second place after the original program. I was developing a bad case of déjà vu; it was me against Viktor in the free skate one more time, and winner takes the Worlds.

The night of my original program was not a happy time.

The pairs had completed their free-skate program, and Canada had reason to celebrate, with Isabelle and Loyd taking a silver medal. But my evening was not full of celebration, because Tuffy and Doug had had a rough skate that night. There were a lot of emotions flaring, and the three of us sat in the hotel room and talked.

With all of this emotion and excitement around me, it was very difficult to get my sleep. I woke up the next day unable to function. I was totally drained, so tired I barely knew where I was. I certainly didn't know what day it was. My first thought was, "Oh, no! I have to skate the exhibitions." Then I woke up a bit more and thought, "You idiot. You haven't even skated the free skate!" Well, yes. Here you have a glimpse of a skater in total command of himself, about to tackle a do-or-die contest with his Russian nemesis, under the firm impression that he'd already done so and could waltz around at the post-competition gala.

It won't surprise you to learn that I arrived at morning practice in a fairly giddy mood. I didn't wear an outfit, just sweat pants and a T-shirt. Most of the other skaters were fully dressed, but I wanted to convey the feeling that they were chasing me, to leave an aura of, "Hey, I've been here before. This is my game now. I've been at the top, and that's where I'm heading again."

I started to joke around with anybody who'd listen. I'd had trouble with my triple Lutz all season, and everybody knew it. Earlier in the week, I'd seen David Dore standing by the boards, and I'd said to him, "I'm going to do a triple Lutz in practice. Give me a day or so, but I'll do one, and I'll dedicate it to you." He laughed, a bit uneasily, I thought. "You know, I'd sure hate to injure myself," I said. "But never mind. I've promised you the Lutz, and you'll get one." Then I started spinning a lurid tale about making it to the Worlds and cracking my back with this crazy Lutz I was honor-bound to attempt. This went on for several days. The morning of the free skate, I skated over to Dore and said, "Look, if you don't mind, I think maybe we shouldn't try this. We've been joking about it, but it's not funny any more. Okay?" "Yeah, yeah," he said. "Maybe we shouldn't do it." "Right. That's a good idea," I said. Then I did a quick circuit of the ice and came around in front of him, watching him squirm as I went to the back outside edge of my blade and landed a faultless Lutz. The look on his face was more than worth the effort.

That afternoon, Trina Driscoll, who used to skate with us at the Royal Glenora, showed up. She was backpacking around Europe, and I went downtown with her and Slipper to see the church and the city hall clock tower, with its life-size figurines that perform to the sound of a glockenspiel. Getting out and seeing the town is always better than sitting in my room on competition day. I got to the rink an hour before I was scheduled to skate and bumped into TV producer John Brunton, wearing his cowboy hat—unlike Dad, who refuses to wear one, for fear that people will think he's overdoing it.

The minute I entered, a posse of cameramen were on my trail. I was talking with Rosemary Marks, our team leader, when Kenny Woo of NBC started filming our conversation. I'd met him in Paris in 1989, and we quickly settled on a good working relationship. He'd go away when I really wanted privacy, and I'd reciprocate by tipping him off when he could grab a really superior shot. "Hey, Kenny," I said. "Why don't you get out of here? I don't mind you guys, but I can't take this for another hour." He laughed and kept on filming. The cameras are always there, and I'd long since learned to deal with them. If you're on a team, sometimes you can hide in the crowd, but when you're skating single, you're out there alone.

I left the ice surface and picked out my place in the dressing room. I'm not seriously superstitious. If I have a good practice, I like to stay in the same spot the next day. If I have a lousy one, I move, and that's about the extent of my irrational beliefs, except for the good-luck guard covers—little cloth socks that slip over my skate guards. My dad's the superstitious member of the Browning family. He likes to find money around the rink, in the parking lot or under his seat. He really feels good about my chances if he turns up a coin or two.

Then it was time to waste some time. I'm expert in this, but not what you'd call consistent. Sometimes I listen to a Walkman, off in the corner by myself. Sometimes I talk with Kristi Yamaguchi, sometimes with Mr. J. Often, he'll come to check on me in the dressing room. He's my link to what's happening out there. He'll poke his head in and say, "Hey, second-last skater in the flight before you is up. Get your outfit on," at which point I start scrambling. It's very reassuring, like having a second alarm clock set.

I used to have trouble deciding when to put my skates on, because my feet seized up when they were laced. Then we worried about retying the laces, about whether or not they were tight enough. This season, though, the problem seemed to mend itself. I'd pull them on whenever I wanted to and just forget about them. After the free skate that day, it felt as if I were wearing running shoes—and thank you, Audi, for the latest job well done.

The more I compete, it seems, the simpler my pre-skate routine becomes. I like to walk out half an hour before my presentation to see the rink, to get a feel for the atmosphere. I'll watch a skater or two; it doesn't matter who they are. I study their jumps, which gets me thinking about my own. Then I return to the dressing room and put on my outfit and skates.

Today, I looked for my family cheering section. They're always there; they never hide in a hotel room watching me on TV. Mom says that she has friends whose kids ride Brahma bulls and are at daily risk of serious injury, and if she couldn't handle watching me skate around in tight pants, she'd consider herself a wimp.

Then I'll do a couple of jumps—a double Axel or a triple toe—simple moves that are almost second nature. I try not to think about the program. Think too much, and the body becomes confused and detached. Think about blinking your eyes, and you won't blink quite so fast.

I stamp my feet and feel the solidity of the blades. Then I go to the boards for a last word with Mr. J. Maybe I've been nursing a bad habit—dropping my arm when I land, finishing the spins with too few revolutions. He'll remind me of it just before I start. All year long, I've been trying to squeeze too much into the end of a program. Even in practice, if I missed a move early on, I'd try to make up for it in the final seconds. Today, Mr. J. said, "If you don't have to repeat anything, if you think you can win without doing something over, don't." Those are a whole lot of words for Mr. J. Usually, he'll say, "Nail it." "Fight." "Work." Today, he was more direct, and I'm glad he said it. I skated away with one aim in mind. I would do my best for four and a half minutes. Then I'd sit and watch Petrenko try to beat me.

Out at center ice, I kept repeating, "Just like practice. One thing at a time. No stopping. Full on it." The opening chords of "Sons of Italy" signaled my start.

I did a triple Axel with kind of an iffy landing, then fought to complete a triple toe-loop. I was angry at myself for not nailing the Axel; proud that I recovered and didn't give up on the toe and turn it into a double. I came around for the quad, far too intent on doing it. I overthought it, perhaps because I'd fallen on an attempt in the warm-up. I didn't pull my arms in tight enough and ended up with a triple. I spent the next few seconds cursing myself, wondering what I could do to compensate. Then I remembered Mr. J.'s advice and thought, "Well, you don't need it. Relax. Enjoy the program." I went through some light footwork, then landed another triple-triple combo.

One of the hardest portions of the program came next—the triple-Axel/double-loop combination. I'd struggled with it all season, because I was trying too hard, jumping off my heel so that my weight stayed back, failing to gain enough height. I was bound and determined not to make that same mistake today, and I succeeded. Off the toe and away—a textbook jump. No problem.

Sometimes, during a free-skating program, I delude myself into thinking that I can save energy in the spins. A tired skater looks for shortcuts. He'll cheat on positions during the spin; he might do the camel and not lay it over. But you don't save energy that way. All you do is demonstrate the fact that you're tired. You convince yourself that you're fading. You shouldn't ever omit an element, especially in a spin, which isn't all that hard to begin with. I have a bad habit of not taking a spin to its full potential. I do it slower than I should; I cheat on the simple moves. I take shortcuts, and it doesn't pay. All these thoughts went through my head as I exited the spin and began some footwork.

Now came the triple-Salchow/triple-loop. It was my best combination, and it looked even better because no one else was attempting it. If I could land it, I'd become the first person to land three triple-triple combos in World competition. Going into it, I thought, "Don't miss this one. This is the clincher."

Maybe this aggressive mindset carried through. I landed it perfectly. Now there wasn't much left—a double Axel and some Russian slits. Flowers rained onto the ice; hundreds of Maple Leaf flags were in motion. I felt satisfied, contented and above all relieved. Satisfied, because

I'd settled a score with Munich's Olympic Hall. In 1988, during a show-tour stop, I'd fallen twice on slushy ice and come off with both costume and ego soaking wet. I'd had bad memories of that ice ever since. Contented, because I'd done the best I knew how. Eight of the nine judges had given me 5.9 for technical performance. For artistic impression, there were four 5.9s and five 5.8s. Relieved, because half the wait was over. But that relief was partial and momentary. The official results were half an hour away. Now it was time to step back and watch Petrenko try to surpass one of the finest performances of my career. This was not beyond his capabilities.

We'd shaken hands before the warm-up began. Each knew the other would do his best. Neither of us would have wanted it any other way. I have the utmost respect for Viktor. For the last three years he's always been there, dogging my footsteps, right behind me at every turn. Russians are fond of nicknames. He calls me "Kurtinka." I can remember a party at Boitano's house in San Francisco when we sat eating shish kebab and laughing. In Halifax, we played video games together before the free skate. He's given me Soviet T-shirts and badges. There's never been a snide or ugly edge to our rivalry. He wants so badly to be world champion. And he deserves to be. He's very, very good.

Now he took his chance. I watched him as he assumed his position at center ice. The only part of his program that I thought might give him trouble was the triple loop. During practice, he seemed to be entering it awkwardly; sometimes he missed it altogether. So I watched him closely as he went into the air. Sure enough, he stepped out of it—he didn't land solidly, under complete control. Your upper body keeps going, pulls you off the foot you land on. You lurch forward and have to keep your balance by falling onto the other foot. I thought, "Okay. I blew the quad. Now you've blown your landing. One mistake, one mistake. We're even."

Then, for an odd reason, I stopped watching. It wasn't because I couldn't bear to watch. On the contrary, I felt fine. But I'd noticed a mountain of flowers, thrown by the Canadian fans, piled all over the table and chairs where Viktor would sit and wait for his marks. I thought, "Oh, no. This is terrible. He'll come off, and maybe he'll have won or maybe he'll have lost—we'll all know in about two and a half minutes—but either way, he shouldn't have to sit there in my flowers." So I started picking them up, but I was running out of time. I started getting mad at people, asking them to give me a hand. I swept them out of camera range and got the area more or less in order. Meanwhile, the cameras were capturing my Mr. Fix-It routine. Lord knows what the reporters thought of me; I think my behavior influenced their questioning, which was at its best. For example: "You wiped your brow when you saw Viktor skating? Was that because you were nervous?" Well, no. It was hot and I was sweating and I'd just realized that I had to dispose of two tons of flowers.

Then Viktor's marks came up. Everyone looked and waited. It seemed as if we waited forever. I think it was actually fifteen or twenty seconds. I've never been really swift at tabulating marks. I don't immediately think, "Oho! Two 5.7s, six judges to three, and away we go." I looked at the CBC booth. No response. I looked at Mr. J. He said, "I'm not sure." Then there was a flurry in the booth, and somebody made a thumbs-up sign—an encouraging gesture, but not a definitive one. I thought, "Well, that could mean Good Skate, or You've Won." People told me later that I looked as if I was in a state of shock. Actually, I was in a state of unfolding confusion, trying to stay cool, guarding against all eventualities. Then Brian Williams nodded his head and Herbie Eisler started cheering. That's when I knew I'd made it.

It's always strange and anti-climactic. It's not like a baseball game—the winning run crosses home plate and it's game over. It's not like hockey—the puck goes in, the red light comes on and it's instant gratification time. In skating, you sit around waiting for nine people to send you conflicting signals. All three times I've won, I've sat there feeling calm, collected and strangely empty.

I react instantly to other people's wins. When Kristi Yamaguchi won the women's championship two days later, I broke into tears on the spot. As a matter of fact, I started to get emotional the second her music began to play. I just can't do it for myself. I go easy on both laughter and tears, because I know exactly how the other skaters feel. I empathize with them. Viktor was visibly disappointed on the podium, which made it difficult for me to jump up and down, even if I'd wanted to. You don't crow when your friend is in obvious distress.

Mom and Dad had an even harder time of it. The family cheering section was out in force this time—Dena and her husand Dan, Wade and his girlfriend Coleen, my cousin Jennifer, my cousin Debbie (who lives in Munich) and her husband Phil, my little cousin Lisa and our friend Tina Wilkins, the London-based Kurt Browning archivist. None of them could figure out what was happening. Dan was watching the CBC booth through binoculars. He said, "Those guys are really ho-hum up there. I don't think Kurt's taken it." Viktor's marks went up, but went down again very quickly. Dena said to Mom, "If the white shirt comes out first for the medal presentation, it's Kurt. If the silver shirt comes out, it's Petrenko." Mom knew very well what color shirt I was wearing and didn't think Dena was being informative. Everyone had to sit through the last four skaters—the better part of half an hour—before the presentations. They didn't know I'd won, and neither did most of the crowd. When I skated out from the corridor, the place went wild.

A lot of skaters feel that standing on the podium is their moment, the high point of the event. But I enjoy my connection with the audience, hearing them sing "O Canada," watching the looks on their faces. I'm happy for them, but I'm more or less under control. Orser, for example, was very emotional on the podium, but I'm not overcome. When I get off the ice and leave the arena by myself, when I'm away from everybody, that's when I get excited.

In Munich, though, my mind was going off in several directions at once. I thought back on the last two wins. In Paris, I didn't know what I'd done. I felt almost apologetic. ("Hey, I didn't mean to do it.") In Halifax, I was thankful, as if I'd reached the surface of the water and could breathe again. This time, I wondered what it meant, and what it was supposed to mean. What would the repercussions be? How would people feel about it? A whole lot of shock waves emanate from that reviewing stand, like ripples in a pond. Millions of people had been sitting in their homes, wishing me well or ill. What did they think about me now?

Then I had a lot of concern for Viktor. I thought, "This is the last straw. I've definitely made an enemy of this Russian guy." The look on his face was incredibly intense. I used to watch him perform throughout the season and think, "If we're skating like this now, what are the Worlds going to be like?" In Munich, I wondered whether the next time around could possibly be any tougher.

And then there were other things to think about. The medal is only the beginning. I still have doping. I still have endless interviews. In Paris, I was so eager to find out what the world champion did. I thought a door would swing wide, and when I walked through it, I could do whatever I wanted. Instead, I sat in an almost deserted arena in the middle of the night, talking to people thousands of miles away. That sounds (to quote Dan) pretty ho-hum, but it's the truth.

I think my attitude toward winning is an extension of the fact that—as I've said—I'm a very practical skater. And being practical has paid off. I've been on the podium most every time I've competed. It's become the logical conclusion; I can almost count on it; I've gotten used to it. This cold-blooded side to my skating personality is very useful. In a way, I find it just as fascinating, just as rewarding, to get ready for and take part in the competition. I'm just as proud of that as I am of winning. So winning isn't some mystical grail. It isn't everything. It's just the end result if I do everything right. Maybe that's why I can win, and the others can't.

I was hoping that Petr Barna would take a medal, because we'd been friends a long, long time. He's been around; he could have used a win. But he skated well, finishing fourth behind Todd Eldredge. Chris Bowman came fifth, followed by Elvis and Slipper. It was a great day for Canada, and an indication of even better days to come.

Brenda Gorman, the CFSA's media liaison, led me down to the doping room. I wanted to make my escape as soon as possible, so I'd been knocking back copious amounts of water and orange juice from the second I left the ice. Two beers later, I was out of there and back into the media scrum.

I didn't mind. Everything is better when you win. Hearing "Congratulations" 150 times sure beats "Gee, I'm really sorry." The first can numb you out; the second is unbearable for all concerned.

Back in my room, Slipper and Kevin Albrecht had started a private party. Kevin is usually quiet and self-contained. This time, he was doing the "Dance of Joy." The hotel management had sent up a six-litre bottle of champagne. I could barely lift it. I phoned Monique in Toronto, then started dialing Caroline numbers before I realized that half the town was in attendance. Then we joined the mainstream party. I found David Dore and handed him my medal. "There you go," I said. "That makes three of them. Medals, medals, medals."

Slipper and Elvis helped me pop the champagne cork—it put a dent in the ceiling. We didn't waste a drop. We went around filling everyone's glass. My extended family, including my cousin Jennifer, had arrived, along with other skaters' parents, CFSA personnel and the Canadian judges. Several speeches later, we headed off in search of another party, carting the bottle of champagne.

At 6:00 in the morning, we were hanging around a pizza stand, arguing about who liked or hated anchovies and pouring champagne for curious passersby. Then we caught a cab back to the hotel and pulled up at 6:30 on the dot. I stepped onto the curb as another cab pulled up behind ours. Its door opened to unload Viktor Petrenko.

We didn't say a lot. All we did was look at each other and smile.

12

INSIDE MY SPORT

Once upon a time, I met an elderly gentleman who
changed the way I look at skating. His name was Walter.
I'm not sure how old he was, but he skated far better than
anyone his age had a right to. Maybe he was ageless; there
was something magical about him. He skated for pleasure,
and he was a pleasure to watch. He was always upright,
hands out and head up. He told me that was the only way
to skate: you had to be ready to bend down and pick up a
stick or a leaf on the ice; you had to be alert for cracks,
ready to protect yourself if you fell. But I never saw him
fall, not even once. He was almost stately in his ways, and
extremely graceful. He opened up my sport—something I
thought I knew all about—and made me wonder what
kind of magic he'd made when he was young. He'd been
skating for fifty years. He'd tapped into and retained the

essence of why people love to skate. It wasn't medals or triple Axels or jumps. It was pure love of an art form. Every once in a while, when I'm competing and things are down, I tend to forget that.

Why am I happy when I step on the ice with my friends? Why do I have so much fun? Because skating is magic. It's one thing Walter taught me that I hope I never forget. It was his magic that I tried to capture in a tribute to him during my TV special "Tall in the Saddle."

The feeling I have for skating is kind of like being in a love-hate relationship. Every time I step on a different patch of ice, I'm a different person, and yet the feeling remains the same. I love the spontaneity, the fact that you can be outwardly smooth while inside, there's so much aggression and power. You can think about it scientifically, analyze the jumps six ways from sundown, do computer simulations. But there are days when I feel as if nothing on earth can knock me over, and it's not scientific any more. It's just freewheeling. There's no premeditation, just speed and power and fun. It's hard to draw on that feeling when you need to—say, at the Worlds. But when you do, and it works, it's as if there ought to be a rule that says: You should not have this much fun. Those days, I connect with the joy of it. No rules, no restrictions.

When I first started skating, I think the idea was simply to stay on the ice and have fun, to see how many people I could meet and how much trouble I could get into. Then I started learning dances and getting a couple of jumps. Gradually, the whole thing changed. I found myself travelling and making new friends, finding out what skating would bring to me. On good days, it was fun. On bad days, I had to find out what I could bring to skating.

A memorable moment for me came in Paris during practices for the 1989 Worlds. I had just seen Viktor Petrenko pull off an incredible triple-Axel/triple-toe combination, and in the bus on the way back to my hotel I started talking about it with my good friend and our team leader, Sally Rehoric, a very generous, very thoughtful woman. We got talking about the physical and emotional excitement of skating—the jumping, flying and spinning—and talking with her brought out ideas that must have been running through my head ever since I got involved in my sport. Late that night, as I lay awake, I turned over these thoughts in my mind.

It all begins with the skates themselves, and the power they contain. I can remember my first skates—and my first bruised knees. That's the beginning of respect. I remember discovering what the picks were for—with enough speed, you could skate at the board and run right up to the top of them, like a squirrel running up a tree, if the maintenance people didn't catch you!

The feeling of jumping is something you can't really describe. You can only hope the audience will catch the feeling by watching you do it. The feeling of a perfectly executed quad is something only a few people in the world know, but it's not the physical sensation that matters as much as the satisfaction you feel—unleashing so much power and yet sustaining control, like jumping a horse. It could be like the follow-through of a throw, or the instinctive satisfaction of throwing and nailing the target—it has to be a very hard throw and a target you didn't really expect to hit.

I feel so comfortable when I watch someone and believe that they have truly found their calling. I feel that sureness when I skate, and that may be why winning is really just the after-effect of skating, not something that should be worried about before you step out on the ice.

That night, I got up and wrote these ideas in a letter to Sally. It helped me focus my own mind, and I hope she understood what I was trying to say.

OTHER VOICES:

David Dore

Kurt is a carefree person. I feel I can say anything to him, but I find I have very little to say to him about his skating per se. He doesn't have a cut-and-dried training schedule. He's unconventional that way. But when we bring our world team members together for the annual seminars, and we run the fitness tests, his results are usually better than those of the others. He never lets himself get out of condition.

An outsider might think he has no concept of how to use his time. He might come across as scattered. But he knows what he's doing. He slots his time perfectly. He focuses in on something, gets it over with, and then his mind is slotting into something else, whether it be practicing or having a construction crew rip up his floor.

Kurt and I tend not to have long conversations. You don't have long conversations with Kurt. You have brief but meaningful conversations.

What he's accomplished over the past four years is quite amazing. In Paris, the feeling was, "Well, let's get out there and see what happens." Halifax was a chance to prove to himself and others that he could recapture the world championship despite adversity. Munich will be remembered for the triple-triple combination jumps. At Albertville, I believe that he will strive to give us all something to remember.

This sport hinges on moments. You don't become world champion because of all the time you've spent thinking about becoming champion. You succeed because—at the moment when you have to be at your best—you produce your best performance. Kurt knows how to do this.

When Kurt went to Paris, I don't think that anybody expected him to be world champion. But I believed that he

172

would win. He fell behind in the figures, and people said, "He can't win now." I said, "No. He knows exactly what he has to do."

To me, Halifax was the turning point of his career. He'd had a dreadful season. This was also the era of skepticism that followed after Ben Johnson. So there was Kurt—in our own country—with the press saying over and over that he could not win again. But he knew how important this competition would be. He had to succeed in Halifax if he was going to leave a mark on the sport.

A lot of people don't realize how much was riding on his free skate that day. But if you look at a tape, and stop it right at the end of the free skate, you can see the look on his face and the way he threw his arm in the air. It's as if he was saying, "Okay, that's that. Now you are going to see me do something in figure skating." He must have thought he'd reached the top of the mountain—that he could determine where he was heading from that moment on. Halifax was where the road to Albertville began.

Kurt's success is founded on phenomenal natural talent. His feet can do amazing things. He can be off balance and out of control, but his feet know how to get him where he has to go. He has extended the technical realm of skating beyond anyone's expectations. Now, he also wants to extend his interpretations. He is not an artistic skater. He is an interpretive skater. I don't think he pretends to be a major artistic talent. He's in the vein of Scottie Hamilton—lively and bouncy and athletic.

What makes Kurt's story intriguing is that it's quite a simple story, quite a simple situation. There's no vast entourage, no bevy of handlers. That's the beauty of it all. People are looking for complexities here, but they just aren't to be found.

So here I am, a three-time world champion. People ask me, "What's your basic, average day?" Of course, there's no such thing. Let me give you an example of how quickly my life has turned upside-down. In 1988, I stood in line—camped in line, really, with blankets and a picnic cooler—to get tickets for an Edmonton Oilers game. I waited from 1:30 at night until 11:00 the following morning and came within thirteen places of getting a seat when the ticket booth opened. In 1989, I dropped the puck at the Oilers–L.A. Kings Stanley Cup opener.

When I was in Munich, Glen Sather, the Oilers' president and general manager, sent a message to my hotel asking me to be the honorary captain. He said the team didn't care if I won or lost; they wanted me regardless. He said they were proud of me, no matter how I made out.

During the last Stanley Cup playoffs, the Oilers brought in a planeload of players from their Cape Breton farm team, and I practiced with them for two weeks. I had a spot in the dressing room, a sweater with my name on the back and sticks with my name on the shafts. The players treated me like one of them, with one exception: they were under sentence of death if they hurt me. I didn't get hurt, and my slap shot improved enormously. More important, when I was on the ice with them, *they* were the special people. I felt so normal, so relieved not to be Kurt Browning, Champion Figure Skater. I was just a guy with a hockey stick in his hands, surrounded by other guys who were far better at what they did than I could ever hope to be.

I've noticed a funny thing. If I do something in public, like participate in a charity softball game, and it's been advertised that I'm going to be there, I can count on spending a lot of my time signing autographs and answering questions about my skating career. But if I drop in to play a few innings with my friends on a local slow-pitch team, there may be just as many people there who recognize me and know who I am, but they'll treat me no differently than anyone else. They are the same people who might ask for an autograph if they saw me at the rink, but they'll recognize that I'm there unofficially—I'm not on stage—and they're willing to forget, for that day, that I'm supposed to be a big deal. I like that.

Usually I can go back to Caroline, of course, and sort of blend in with the scenery—unless they've decided to roll out the red carpet. They've done it for me twice. The last event, immediately after Munich, was a record-breaker. I forget how many autographs I signed. There was a hayride, then a ceremony at the arena. To tell the truth, I was nervous. Sitting at the head table, I felt as if I were getting married. I started concentrating very hard, so as to remember everyone I ever went to school with and his little brother, who when I last saw him was three-foot-eight, and now he's six-foot-two. As usual, Dad put things in perspective. "It's their party, not yours," he said. "You just enjoy it."

So I did. There were fifty Canadian flags and well over a thousand people coming and going. The whole thing was beautifully planned; the food was tremendous. They presented me with gifts. People arrived from all the surrounding towns, having organized their schedules around me. I must have shaken hands with half the province. I danced with my mom and my niece. I had a beer with some of my old buddies in the quietest corner we could find. They sat there, saying things like, "I can't believe what's happened to you, that you do what you do." Mom kept trying to slow me down; sometimes she says I try to give too much. That night—as always—Caroline gave me more than I can ever repay.

And then, at three-thirty in the morning, I cranked up the famous VW Beetle and headed for Edmonton airport, to fly to Toronto and co-host a Kids Help Phone Telethon. Another basic, average day was under way.

The Kids Help Phone is a good idea, and I've given them a hand the past few years. It's a 1-800 number that any kid—usually, teenagers—can call if they're in distress and need somebody to talk to. Then there's the Muscular Dystrophy Telethon, and another for Literacy Canada. I'm a real asset to these things. They can count on me to keep on babbling, no matter what the hour.

I've also skated—along with Orser, Hamilton and Cranston—in special Stars on Ice shows to benefit Ronald McDonald Children's Charities, which provide houses where out-of-town families can stay if their kids are being treated in big-city hospitals. They also provide equipment for the hospitals themselves. I didn't know how I'd feel about going to the hospitals, because some of these kids are in rough shape, and I'm no Mother Teresa. The odd thing is, I feel really comfortable when I'm with them. Maybe they're in wheelchairs; maybe they've never caught a baseball or run down the hallway, and maybe they never will. But boy, are they fighting hard. There aren't any medals for that kind of competition, but I think a pretty good start would be to play the national anthem each time one of these kids leaves the hospital.

The other question people ask me is: What's next? So let's talk about that for a while. I warn you, I'm not real good at crystal balls, but I'll give it a try.

Seven years ago, if you'd asked me about the future of figure skating, I certainly wouldn't have said: me. So any prediction is probably doomed to failure. Skating grows and changes like any other sport. Rules keep changing, to keep pace with our abilities. And there's a bigger audience to please; that's why compulsory figures had to go. If people had wanted to watch them, we'd still be doing them. I suspect that someday even the name will change. "Figure skating" doesn't adequately describe what's going on out there.

I hesitate to predict what's going to happen in competition in the immediate future. If I say "No one will ever succeed in doing such-and-such," you can bet it will happen, six months down the line. At some point, though, you hit the outside of the envelope. There are practical limitations on what the human body can do.

I think there'll probably be a quintuple jump—a quint—five revolutions in full flight. I don't think I'll be the one to land it, but every day, I see kids who spin so fast it makes me dizzy. One of them will make it. Skates are getting better; bodies are getting stronger; skaters are starting younger. Five is the limit, but five is just around the corner.

Four revolutions—the quad—will become old hat. Six or seven guys will attempt it. There'll probably be a quad Axel; I'm working on quad Salchows now. There will be more than one quad in a program. There'll be quad-double or quad-triple combinations. We know these things will happen because of what's taken place the past two or three years. In the 1988 Olympics, Orser's free skate contained seven or eight triple jumps. Only two were in combination—a triple-triple and a triple-double. In Munich, I did eight triples in combinations—three of them triple-triples—and considered doing the quad. That's not to say that Orser or Boitano couldn't have done what I did, simply that they didn't have to in order to win.

The era of Orser and Boitano was a blend of artistry and athleticism. Now it seems as if there's no time to be artistic. You have to do extraordinary things to keep pace. It's become a crapshoot—all or nothing. It's also become quite high-risk. If you stop to think about it, we should be wearing helmets; we're doing dangerous stuff. It's a wonder that more skaters aren't seriously hurt. It may take a serious injury to slow things down, so that the pendulum swings back toward a greater emphasis on quality programs.

You have to cover all the bases. You can't do nothing but jump; you can't indulge in nothing but long, meaningful arabesques and glides. You have to satisfy both the technical and artistic sides. I'd like to see separate judges for each category. That way, they'd mark only their area of expertise;

177

they wouldn't have two sets of marks to play with. This would dramatically increase the cost of mounting a competition, but it would be far more fair to the competitors.

I'd also like to see a World Cup skating circuit. It would be far more interesting for the fans if they could watch a whole series of competitions, with points awarded and prize money distributed, to determine who will be the world's best skater in any given year.

The skaters would be forced to live out of a suitcase, it's true. But how long are we at our competitive peak? Not very many years. If the circuit paid enough money—and it would, given TV rights and sponsorships of every kind—I think we'd be willing to attempt it. I could see skaters seizing the agenda here, getting this off the ground by means of a consensus among ourselves. After all, it would simply be an extension of what we're already doing. We're constantly going to competitions. If the season were extended, we'd simply have to stay in shape a little longer. The World Cup and the Worlds wouldn't conflict. Rather, they'd co-exist. There's room for both of them.

The thing that bothers some people about world competition at the moment is that it's absolutely do-or-die. That's stimulating, sure. It gets the adrenalin flowing. But not only is there no second chance—no element of best two out of three—but the differences that determine who's world champion and who's not are almost insanely minute. At the Calgary Olympics, Orser lost to Boitano by one-tenth of a point. What does that mean? What can it mean? At that stage, the system itself loses meaning. Surely it would be more fair to all concerned if champions were chosen by means of cumulative scores, arrived at in competitions scattered over a longer time period, held under all sorts of conditions. That way, a whole season's work wouldn't be destroyed by one tiny, fractional lapse.

Whatever the next breakthroughs are going to be, I'm glad to say that many will very likely happen in Canada.

Per capita, we're the best skaters in the world, for several reasons. First of all, success breeds success. When I was working my way up from novice to junior to senior, who were my role models? They were silver and gold medal-winners, world champions, people of remarkable accomplishment. I followed immediately behind Brian Orser. Those are pretty tough boots to fill, but I was encouraged by the fact that he'd filled them. My expectations of what it took to be a Canadian champion were high. To be Canadian champion, you have to skate incredibly well. The competition is fierce. If you beat it, you've already beaten some of the world's best, so you're virtually assured a shot at the top-ten placement at the Olympics, or Worlds. You go in thinking, "Hey! I'm the Canadian. Look at me." You're justifiably proud, and you aren't apt to settle for anything less than your best.

Now, compare this to the experience of a British skater. He may have won the British championship, but his competition wasn't nearly as tough. He had an easier time of it. That's not callous, it's the truth. It doesn't mean that a unique individual from Britain or Australia might not beat the Canadian. But, as a general rule, it will be harder for him. A Canadian, on the other hand, is all fired up. Canadians look back to Donald Jackson, Barbara Ann Scott and Petra Burka. They measure themselves against these stellar reputations. They look back to Orser; maybe now they look to me. Canadian skaters—both boys and girls—can logically hope to reach the very highest level. It's been done; it's attainable. That man and that woman did it. Therefore the kid from Smalltown, Anyprovince, can do it, too.

Remember also that the Canadian system—which has produced all these success stories—will make the most of that kid's talent. We have David Dore's national team, the training camps, the seminars, the high-caliber coaching in every part of the country. Young skaters of promise are identified early on. They learn a bit of everything—how to

179

handle the press, how to do a proper drug test, how to present themselves with poise. They meet senior skaters from across the country; they meet athletes from other fields. They train together, compare notes together. The system isn't hit-or-miss. It's the envy of the world. It produces excellence. It moulds the best skaters. And it will continue getting better. The best is yet to come.

Michael Jiranek

What is next for Kurt? You can't predict. He is such a unique case. But we can look to other sports. He may perhaps be a commentator. I think he'll be active in some way in both sport and public life.

As for turning professional, I don't consider professional skating a career. He won't be doing it when he is forty-five. I don't think that he'd make a good coach—he's not patient enough. He's impatient with himself. A coach must be patient and listen to other people. Kurt is very excitable, a very life-enjoying person. Physically very skilled. Contrary to what many people believe, he's a hard worker.

In the immediate future, there are a few things I think he will accomplish. For example, the quad Salchow. It wouldn't surprise me; he is capable of doing it. But he may not have time to practice this one element. It's so hard to achieve. By the time you work on the choreography, the spins, you have very little energy or strength left to work on the most difficult element. If you spend all your energy perfecting that element, then suddenly the easier elements aren't so easy any more. So you must find more energy,

180

more time to work on something else. In that way, it will be very difficult to push much further the abilities of skaters to achieve more. Not that they won't be strong enough, but it takes so much time, so much top concentration. Then you fall, over and over, hundreds and hundreds of times. Your body can take only so much beating, so much punishment.

One hesitates to say that there are finite limits, because we have improved so many times. But we shall see.

OTHER VOICES:

Kevin Albrecht

When and if Kurt turns professional is yet to be decided. Everyone has assumed that in 1992, having hopefully won his fourth world championship and done well at the Albertville Olympics, he will retire from competitive skating. The press is virtually counting down to this, and Kurt himself has made statements along these lines. Lately, however, we have been considering the fact that the next Olympics—in Lillehammer, Norway—will take place in 1994, instead of 1996, as would usually be the case. Two years go by very quickly. This has made us step back and reconsider. The questions are: Does Kurt want to go on from a skating perspective? and What are the financial implications?

Oddly enough, Kurt could probably make more money by remaining an amateur until 1994 than he would were he to turn pro in 1992. He would lose out, because his sponsors might not be there, due to the fact that he wouldn't have the Canadian Maple Leaf on his back. He wouldn't be competing on the world stage for Canada.

181

As a result, he would imperil his corporate endorsements. We would negotiate other deals, and he would make appreciable sums from the tours. But he can do better financially by continuing with the sponsors we now have, and by skating in tours organized around him, which he headlines.

At the 1994 Olympics, if he chooses to compete, Kurt will be only twenty-seven. He certainly won't be over the hill. On the contrary, he should be at his peak. Orser, for example, was twenty-eight in Calgary. Remember also that Kurt is way ahead of schedule. He wasn't supposed to start winning as early as he did. Because he's three-time world champion, people think, "Well, time for him to start thinking about something else." Not necessarily, because he started so young.

As far as the purely business side goes, I think that Kurt has taken figure skating to a new level. I hope that younger skaters will recognize this and look upon him as the guy who broke the ground. He spent a good deal of money in legal fees to ensure that an athlete has the right to control his or her trust fund. No one will have to go through that process again. There's a standard agreement now. When Josée Chouinard, Elvis Stojko or other young skaters want it, it's there. All they'll have to do is fill in the blanks.

I think that skating will change quite radically in the next decade, going the way of alpine skiing and tennis. Professional staffs will take over from volunteers. Eventually, there'll be a World Cup circuit of figure-skating competitions—a world skating tour. There'll be a skating commissioner, just as there are football and baseball commissioners. Maybe that will be Kurt.

Whatever Kurt decides to do, I know he will do it with energy and passion. Kurt is a very talented person who has the great ability to perform under pressure. He has taken advantage of the opportunities given to him and gone through it all with a smile on his face. It is a privilege to both work professionally with Kurt and call him a friend.

On a day-to-day basis, I'm not the best role model in the world. Parents are unlikely to point to me and say to their champions of tomorrow, "This is the ideal way to behave. Act just like Kurt, and you are bound to win." I've never been on a real weight-lifting program, and when I work out it's disguised as tennis or bike riding. I'm not the all-purpose super-athlete. I walk around wearing cutoff shorts, a rock-band T-shirt and running shoes that should have been thrown out a long time ago. I eat nachos in the lounge. I drink beer and go to parties and sometimes drive cars too fast. I don't get caught up in being somebody's everything, everyday. If I tried to do that—or if I tried to tell myself that's what I was—I'd go crazy. But I am a person who believes in doing the right thing, who tries to do it, who has achieved what he's achieved through hard work and honest desire. I'm proud of that. And if people can't see that, I think they're looking at me the wrong way.

I get slam mail sometimes, along the lines of "Who do you think you are?" Well, I'm probably not who the writer thinks I am. By assuming I'm something, by having that preconception in mind, that writer's being unfair. I can't live up to these expectations, good or bad. I know it's tough not to have preconceptions about someone who's always in the newspapers or on TV. People think, "Holy cow! He must be rich. Is he ever high on himself" and so forth. I don't know what else they think, but if they ever get a chance to meet me, I would hope they approach me with an open mind. That probably goes for anybody you've already met through the eyes of the media.

When I compete, I'm an opportunist. Every competitor has to be. That's the way things are. We have to find out who's better, who's the best. Is that what the Worlds and the Olympics are all about? Do they really prove who is the best? They're still going to pick someone to be the the best skater in the world on that particular day, so I take advantage of that situation. I relish it. I like the fact that we're pitted against each other. It's not life or death, but there's still that element of high-stakes confrontation. Not everyone can compete at this level. I can. It's an opportunity, and I've accepted it.

Do I have regrets? Not the ones you might think—leaving school at an early age, dedicating myself to skating all my life. Whatever I gave up for skating I got back tenfold. I had a great time growing up, a family who supported me all the way. I did what I loved to do, and I was good at it. I've reaped rewards beyond my wildest dreams. I wasn't pushed or dragged into anything, by my parents, my coach or anyone else.

There are things other skaters do that I can't, that I'm envious of. I envy Boitano's absolute ability to do jumps, Scottie Hamilton's ability to maintain momentum, his speed and acceleration, the way he lands and looks as if he's still flying. I envy Orser's belief in his every move. I envy Gary Beacom's ability to sidestep all the rules, all the norms of skating, and do what he wants to do.

When I cease to compete, and I don't have to satisfy the judges any more, my skating style may move toward something more personal. Even now, I try to tap into what the people want on a given night and become what they want me to be. I'm reading them, responding to the message. This crowd has a sense of humor; that one wants something mildly risqué, a flirtatious move, leaping into the stands to kiss the girls. So I'm a showman, playing to the audience. I love the crowd, even when they don't clap in time! Eventually, this side of my skating personality will assume a greater importance. You can't measure showmanship in tenths of a point, and I find that prospect very appealing.

I'm a very logical kind of skater. I try to simplify things as much as possible. I don't like deep, convoluted ideas. That's why I like the visualization process in theory, and I must admit it's worked for me on several occasions. Peter Jensen, a friend and sports psychologist, would say, "All right. Let's step back and look at what you're doing." Well and good. But I've seen other skaters who went overboard. When someone starts finding more problems than you knew you had, it's time to call a halt. I like to get on the ice and try my best to win. Then I can go home.

It's easy to get carried away and lose sight of what you're doing. Skaters are of earth-shattering importance for a couple of days a year. Then we disappear for a bit, while people watch baseball and get on with their lives. The world championships are important, but so is a child's birthday party. So is Christmas. So are the Olympics. We look forward to these things so much. Once they're over, we start counting down to the next time—only 360 days until the next May long weekend.

I'm counting down now to the Albertville Olympics. I'm glad I have Calgary under my belt. At the Worlds, I don't walk in with three hundred other athletes all wearing the same colors. A viewer can't say, "Yes! That's my flag. I can identify with this." At the Olympics, we put our pride on the line. There's an element of: "If I win the Worlds, I'm the best. If I win the Olympics, *we're* the best." I understand that. I get excited watching the Stanley Cup. I get mad if the Edmonton Oilers lose. So I can't blame people for getting mad at me.

In order to prevent this from happening, I plan to keep on getting better. I don't think I'm as good as I'm going to get. I'd like to think my peak as a skater is yet to come. Orser and Boitano are skating as well now as they did at the Calgary Olympics, and artistically, they're so much better. When I stop getting better, I'll have run out of this tank of gas, and it'll be time to go and do something else.

I accept all the things—good and bad—that come with skating. I fall down, I hurt, I have enough stitches in me to sew up a baseball, I answer the same questions over and over. That's not so great. But I get to travel, meet fascinating people, do interesting things, and I'm world champion. That's pretty good. If I harped on the downside, I might stop. Then I'd have to put up with something else.

Skating has its rewards. I've owned a little era. And even if it all stopped tomorrow, I'd have my own two legs, I could hug my mom and dad, and I could sit on the porch in Caroline and replay interesting memories. The only conclusion is that it's been a wonderful way to go, and it's still wonderful, day by day.

I love sitting around a table with friends hearing good stories, and I hope you've enjoyed hearing some of mine. If I've told them right, you may feel you've touched a part of my highs, lows and in-betweens. If I happen to fall on my face next time out, it's not going to be the end of the world. It will be one day of my life. I've told you about the times I placed fifth or eleventh or sixteenth. Those were three days of my life. They weren't real great, but the world didn't end. That's why Mr. J. says, "We're going to do what you can do today." Today isn't last year. It's just today.

Today, I'm still world champion. I've been at the top for three years. There'll be a time when I'm not there any more. I'll deal with that when it happens. I was doing fine without the fame, and I'll do fine when it ends.

I hope that, now you've read this book, you know a little bit more about me and my skating. Before I step off the ice, I want to leave an impression with the audience. I want to make them feel a little bit better than they did.

And maybe—if I'm really lucky—they'll be in the car after the show and somebody will say, "Do you remember the spot where he did that flip and fell on his back and then wiggled around? That made me laugh. What was your favorite part?" If what I do stays with them longer than the moment, then I've succeeded.

ACKNOWLEDGEMENTS

I love to bring friends home and watch their faces when my mom talks to them. She loves to visit, and she talks to the skaters, media and famous people who pass through our house just the way she talks to me.

The long hours I spent with my parents driving to skating practices really gave us a chance to become friends, and talk, and learn. On special, very early morning trips, there would be an incredible display of Northern Lights, and my mom never hesitated to stop the car and take the time to look. I have never forgotten the importance of what I now call "nature breaks."

Mom has a great, sometimes quirky sense of humor, and when she teases me—like warning what she would do to me if she ever found one of my autographs that she couldn't read—she's also teaching me lessons. Simple things, but with meanings that last. Mom, I can't thank you enough.

It was great growing up with your father a cowboy—actually, part cowboy, part mountain man. My father gave his family a wonderful home, and I feel so proud of my parents' farm and our heritage. My father is a very proud man; it shows in everything he does. If something was broken, it was always fixed, not only that day, but better than before. When he patched the hole in my hockey gloves, I always thought that was his way of saying he cared.

Dad's high standards meant he also had high expectations, so when I rolled his brand-new snowmobile down a hard-packed icy road at forty miles per hour two days before going to the Halifax Worlds, it meant a lot to me when he didn't get too mad. I am forgiven, aren't I?

Agent: the word sends fear into the eyes of most people. Agents have been compared to both angels and hitmen, but I've been lucky. My agents are also friends.

Michael Barnett once said to me, "When you skate at the Olympics, your whole future will *not* be on the line that day!" What he promised me in 1988 was that in four years' time I would actually look forward to stepping on the ice in Albertville, and he was right. I wish I could see more of Mike, but our schedules hardly ever match, and whenever I do see him he has a phone glued to his shoulder. He thinks bigger than anyone I know, and I thank him for opening up my life to so many things I never would have dreamed possible. Believe me, Barney. I'm glad we met.

The man most people associate with the business of Kurt Browning is Kevin Albrecht. Kevin is the one who is there for the press conferences, the interviews, appearances and competitions. (Actually, he has yet to see me compete in person where I have *not* taken the gold medal—a record we would both like to keep alive!)

Kevin is one of the people in my life who I truly trust—in business and in friendship. For my own good, he taught me how to use the word "no" while we were stuck in traffic in a taxi one day. He made me practice it over and over. The driver must have thought we were crazy! I can count on Kevin's advice to take a difficult situation in the right direction. When he talks, I listen, because he always knows what he is talking about, whatever the topic. And if he doesn't know it already, he mysteriously learns it behind your back; that's what happened when he was introduced to the wonderful world of figure skating. Creative ideas never seem to stop coming from Kevin. Oh, and thanks to Kevin's wife, Sally, for putting up with our ridiculous schedule!

Imagine having a job like this: on call all the time for a mad dash to the airport; calls from Europe to wire money; taking care of a house that has a bad habit of flooding; running errands all the time. Since I am out of town and away from home more than I am there, I sometimes abuse my friendship with Gareth Edwards. My best friend away from the skating world is just that—out of this world! He is crazy, laughs at my jokes, and is my best friend. Gareth, the job is still yours if you want it!

Considering how much of what I love about my life exists because of skating, it only makes sense to thank this person. Karen McLean, you are someone that none of us kids from Caroline and Rocky will ever forget. Thank you for the best push-start anybody ever had.

Without all my great teammates, and the friends I've made all over the world, it would all have been meaningless. There are so many memories that can't be contained even in the pages of a book, but all of them are equally important. By the way, that goes for all my friends at the Royal Glenora that I skate with every day. You guys are great!

Thanks to the Edmonton press for putting skating on the front page of the sports section. Thanks especially to Marty Knack and Gordon MacAlpine for their extra work and friendship.

Thanks, too, to Canadian Airlines and Air Canada. They treat me like gold and make traveling a breeze. Canadian has even awarded me honors and free trips.

Finally, thanks to everyone who has ever clapped when I stepped on the ice. You gave me the courage to go for it. Whether I'm warming my hands by the fire in "Bring Him Home" from *Les Miserables* or dancing like a crazy man in my Lyle Lovett number, I'm doing it for you!

KURT BROWNING

Club	Royal Glenora
Training Site	Edmonton, Alberta
Hometown	Caroline, Alberta
Place of Birth	Rocky Mountain House, Alberta
Date of Birth	June 18, 1966
Height	5'7" / 170 cm
Weight	143 lb. / 64.3 kg
Coach	Michael Jiranek

COMPETITIVE RECORD

Domestic

1991 Canadians – 1st
1990 Canadians – 1st
1989 Canadians – 1st
1988 Canadians – 2nd
1987 Canadians – 2nd
1986 Canadians – 5th
1985 Canadians – 1st (jr)
1983 Canadians – 1st (nov)
1982 Canadians – 12th (nov)
1990 Goodwill 1st
1991 Lalaquio 1st
1992 worlds 2nd
1993 canadian 1st
1993 worlds 1st
1993 Skate Am 1st
1994 Canada 2nd
1994 Olympic 5th

International Competitions

1991 Worlds – 1st
1990 Nations Cup – 1st
1990 Skate Canada – 1st
1990 Goodwill Games – 1st
1990 Worlds – 1st
1989 NHK – 3rd
1989 Skate America – 3rd
1989 Worlds – 1st
1988 NHK – 3rd
1988 Skate Canada – 1st
1988 Skate Electric Invt'l – 1st
1988 Worlds – 6th
1988 Olympics – 8th
1987 Skate Canada – 4th
1987 St. Ivel – 2nd
1987 Worlds – 15th
1986 NHK – 7th
1986 Oberstdorf – 3rd
1986 St. Gervais – 2nd
1985 Oberstdorf – 9th
1985 St. Gervais – 2nd

1990 Lou Marsh Award – Canada's Outstanding Athlete
1990 Lionel Conacher Award – The Canadian Press Male Athlete of the Year
1990 Recipient of the "Order of Canada," the country's most prestigious civilian award
1990 Sports Federation of Canada – Top Male Athlete

Kurt has the distinction of being the first athlete in the histroy of figure skating to successfully complete a quadruple jump in World competition. The feat was accomplished at the World Championships in Budapest, Hungary, March 1988. Kurt is also listed in the Guinness Book of World Records for this amazing achievement.

Presents...

KURT BROWNING
"JUMP"

You are now eligible to see KURT BROWNING "IN ACTION" In this exclusive offer

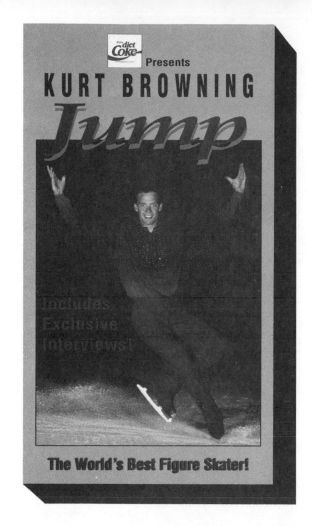

his video biography features one of the world's extraordinary athletic .lents: THE WORLD'S BEST FIGURE SKATER!

JUMP" will take you person-to-person with Kurt Browning and his parents here you'll hear their thoughts about competition and the pressures of .e media.

.cluded is action footage from:

THE 1989 AND 1990 WORLD FIGURE SKATING CHAMPIONSHIPS
THE QUAD: THE FIRST TIME IN HISTORY FOR A SUCCESSFUL QUADRUPLE
JUMP IN COMPETITION - SHOWN HERE IN SUPER SLOW MOTION
THE INTENSE ONE-ON-ONE RIVALRY WITH THE SOVIET UNION'S
BEST, VIKTOR PETRENKO

16.99 per video (GST included)
lus $4.00 postage and handling
Ontario residents add 8% PST)
o order by credit card call
-800-667-KURT / 1-800-667-5878

Or mail a cheque/money order
Payable to: Kurt Browning Video
Unit #1, 480 Tapscott Road
Scarborough, Ontario M1B 1W3